BLOCKCHAIN UNCHAINED: UNDERSTANDING BLOCKCHAIN FROM THE GROUND UP

DR. DEEPAK SUKHEJA
DR. KRITI OHRI
DR. SABBINENI NAGINI
DR. UMESH KUMAR SINGH

notionpress.com

INDIA • SINGAPORE • MALAYSIA

ISBN 979-8-89610-660-9

CONTENTS

BOOK'S BLURB

Title: Blockchain Unchained: Understanding Blockchain from the Ground Up: **An Introductory Textbook on the Future of Decentralized Technology.**

In a society where technology is rapidly changing working environment, blockchain is emerging as one of the most revolutionary innovations of the twenty-first century. But why is blockchain so crucial and exactly what is it?

"Understanding Blockchain Technology" serves as an in-depth introduction to understand the fundamentals of this revolutionary technology. This book provides all knowledge necessary to fully understand blockchain technology. Upon completing this book, readers will be familiar with the intricacies of blockchain technology and its use across several fields. This book encompasses all aspects of blockchain technology, including cryptography, cryptocurrencies, Bitcoin, and the diverse platforms and tools utilized for blockchain development.

- **Explore the origins** of blockchain, starting with its role in cryptocurrencies like Bitcoin and Ethereum.

- **Discover real-world applications** in industries like finance, supply chain management, healthcare, and beyond.

- **Understand key concepts** such as decentralization, smart contracts, and consensus mechanisms.

- **Learn about the future potential** of blockchain, including its role in Web 3.0 and decentralized finance (DeFi).

Author

Dr. Deepak Sukheja
Associate Professor
VNR VJIET Hyderabad

Dr. Kriti Ohri
Assistant professor
VNRVJIET Hyderabad.

Dr. Sabbineni Nagini
Professor
VNR VJIET Hyderabad

Dr. Umesh Kumar Singh
Professor
INSTITUTE OF COMPUTER SCIENCE,
VIKRAM UNIVERSITY, UJJAIN

PREFACE

Blockchain technology stands as one of the excellent technological innovations of the 21st century. Blockchain technology offers transparency, security, and decentralization. An immutable, distributed ledger shifts the dependence away from centralized authorities, creating a novel framework of trust. The fundamental purpose of this book is to provide fundamental knowledge of blockchain technology in its theoretical and practical aspects. This book provides all the necessary information to fully understand blockchain technology. After reading this book, readers will be able to comprehend the inner workings of blockchain technology and apply it to a variety of domains. This book encompasses all aspects of blockchain technology, encompassing cryptography, cryptocurrencies, Bitcoin, and the diverse platforms and tools utilized to construct blockchains.

To comprehend blockchain and its underlying technology, we must go back in time. Remember that blockchain isn't new. Like any other, its construction relied on the ideas of its predecessors. To fully benefit from this book, readers should have a basic understanding of computer science and computer networking experience. If that's not the case, you can still easily read this book, as it provides relevant background material where necessary.

WHY THIS BOOK

Blockchain technology is transforming the way we think about data, trust, and digital interaction. Whether you're intrigued by the potential of cryptocurrencies, exploring decentralized applications (dApps), or looking to future-proof your business, understanding blockchain has become essential. But blockchain is a complex, rapidly evolving field—and this book is here to guide you through it. This book provides a comprehensive understanding of blockchain's ecosystem, avoiding technical details. This is an excellent starting point for both casual learners and aspiring blockchain developers.

WHAT THIS BOOK COVERS

We specifically designed this book with a student mindset, aiming to provide a comprehensive yet approachable guide to blockchain technology. Whether you're studying computer science or simply curious about emerging technologies, this book will give you a thorough grounding in the essentials of blockchain while connecting you to real-world applications and career opportunities.

Chapter 1: The first chapter discusses the fundamentals of blockchain technology. You'll learn about key concepts. It covers blockchain's history, definitions, characteristics, kinds, and benefits. This chapter also discusses the properties of blockchain technology.

Chapter 2: This chapter covered the essential terms and components of blockchain technology, including the structure of a block, the chain of blocks, transactions, the virtual machine, and scripting or programming languages. This chapter additionally discusses the different forms of block mining and the process of transaction validation.

Chapter 3: This chapter explores the operational framework of blockchain technology, emphasizing the key elements of a blockchain network and their respective functions. This chapter further explains the decentralized mechanism of the blockchain application to facilitate secure communication between unknown nodes.

Chapter 4: This chapter outlines the typical architecture found in blockchain applications. This chapter additionally discusses the main categories of blockchain networks or types of blockchain, including public blockchains, private blockchains, consortium blockchains, and hybrid blockchains. This chapter additionally discusses their benefits, drawbacks, and ideal uses.

Chapter 5: This chapter focused on consensus processes in decentralized architecture and consensus algorithms that foster trust in decentralized environments. This chapter also explored various consensus mechanism principles, such as the Byzantine fault **tolerance,** proof of work, proof of stake, etc.

Chapter 6: This chapter described the real-time application (cryptocurrency) of blockchain technology. The topic included an introduction to cryptocurrencies and how they function. The chapter also delved into the topic of bitcoin, including its transactions and the significance of tokens and wallets.

Chapter 7: This chapter focuses on the integration of blockchain technology with other cutting-edge technologies like cloud computing, the Internet of Things, artificial intelligence, and data science.

Chapter – 01

EMERGENCE OF BLOCKCHAIN TECHNOLOGY

Introduction

Blockchain Technology is the focal point of the twenty-first century. As our daily lives require more modernization, we are becoming more receptive to new technologies. Modern technology has become an integral part of our daily lives, from using a remote to control devices to giving instructions through voice notes. In the past decade, technologies such as augmented reality, Artificial Intelligence and IoT have gained momentum in most of application domains. Now, there is a new addition to this group: Blockchain Technology.

Blockchain technology is a revolutionary technology impacting exclusive industries. It has attracted great interest from both academia and enterprise. The generation started out with Bitcoin, a cryptocurrency that has reached a capitalization of one hundred and eighty billion dollars ($829 billion) as of December 2022. According to the authorities' record in 2022, the blockchain technology is receiving billions of dollars in studies and business enterprise investments, and much greater is predicted to return soon. There's a common false impression amongst human beings that Bitcoin and Blockchain are one and the same, but that isn't the case.

Blockchain technology can be used to create cryptocurrencies, and apart from Bitcoin, there are numerous packages which are being evolved on the idea of blockchain technology. The technology currently encompasses a wide range of applications that are both popular and influential in the field of networking research, Healthcare, the Internet of Things (IoT), cloud garages, cloud security, automobility, workplace automation, and the training sector are examples of such projects, among others.

In general, blockchain technology has proven its worth in any application that requires a decentralized non alterable ledger now only and only appendable ledger with the majority of consensus. JP Morgan's

Interbank Information Network, which enables fast, secure, and low-cost international bills, is a good example of how blockchains can be used. In addition, supply chain structures by IBM are exploring the capacity of the usage of blockchains of their offerings aside of that maximum of service-based companies deploying this technology in CRM (customer relationship management).

Bitcoin and the blockchain are not the same. Bitcoin transactions can be recorded and stored on the blockchain, but there are numerous other uses for the technology. Even if Bitcoin is the initial application for blockchain, it is only the beginning.

1.1 Blockchain

Nowadays, blockchain technology is taken into consideration as the most extensive invention on the internet. A blockchain is a secured, shared, and distributed ledger that helps the process of recording and tracking assets without the need for a centralized, trusted authority. It allows two events to communicate and trade assets in a peer-to-peer (P2P) community where distributed choices are made with the aid of most people instead of a single centralized authority. It is provably comfortable in opposition to attackers who attempt to manipulate the gadget by compromising the centralized controller. Resources can be tangible (e.g., cash, homes, vehicles, or land) or intangible (e.g., copyrights, digital documents, and intellectual asset rights). Something valuable can be tracked on a blockchain community to reduce security risks and save all parties involved money on security monitoring.

Blockchain is a new family member of the database management system. It works in a distributed environment. A blockchain can be defined as distributed database that is shared among the nodes of a computer network, and these nodes of computers are connected through peer-to-peer network technology, which leads to the concept of the decentration process. Like a database, a blockchain stores information electronically in a virtual layout. i.e., an advanced type of digitalized record keeping system. Blockchains play a crucial role in cryptocurrency systems like Bitcoin, ensuring a comfortable and decentralized record of transactions. The innovation of a blockchain lies in its ability to ensure the consistency and protection of a record of transactions, thereby generating trust without the need for a trusted third party. The structure of the information distinguishes a blockchain from a normal database. A blockchain collects facts together in activities, referred to as blocks, that hold sets of records. Blocks have certain storage capacities and, while filled, are closed, and linked to the formerly filled block, forming a sequence of facts known as the blockchain.

All of the new statistics that follow the new block are put together into a new block that can then be added to the chain when it's full. In other words, Blockchain is a new member of the database management system family. Like a database, a blockchain stores information electronically in a virtual layout. The innovation with a blockchain is that it ensures the constancy and protection of a record of records. It generates trust without the need for a trusted third party.

A database usually organises its data into tables. A blockchain, on the other hand, organizes its data into chunks (blocks) that can be linked together. This information structure is built to make a timeline of records that can't be reversed even when it's used in a decentralised way. Blocks that are filled become part of this timeline. As each block is added to the chain, it has an exact time stamp.

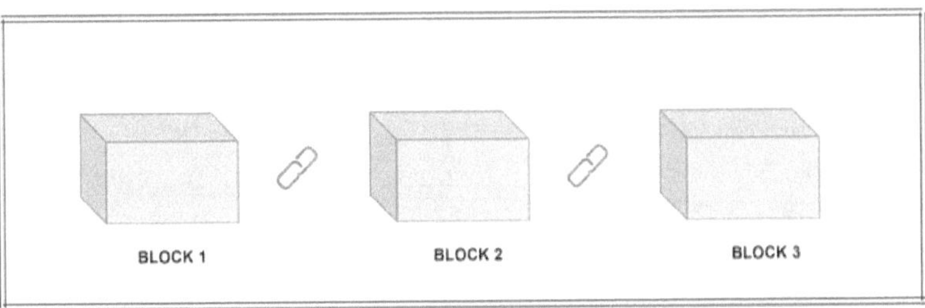

Figure 1.1: A Simple Blockchain Model

The blockchain will keep track of all types of information transfers. This is referred to as a ledger mechanism, and the data transfers are referred to as 'transactions.' Because blockchain is a distributed P2P ledger system, anybody can view the entries of other users, but no one can alter or change them. It improves the overall level of transparency of the device. However, it will not replace the traditional centralised database network used by authorities; rather, it will shape a whole new mechanism in global enterprises. After verification, each transaction is added to the ledger as a block. It uses a exclusive kind of disbursed network to ensure that every transaction is on the factor among P2P nodes. In other words, "Blockchain is a distributed P2P ledger system, anybody can view the entries of other users, but no one can alter or change them. It uses an exclusive kind of disbursed network to ensure that every transaction is on the same level of scrutiny among nodes". Blockchain reduces trust from a single source and distributes it among all nodes in the network. The blockchain is established in a single linked list in a linear way in which the first block is referred to as a **Genesis Block**. The advanced features of blockchain include immutability, which means that once the records are published, they cannot be edited or deleted (to edit the record system need the consensus from all peers). For example, Bitcoin, a distributed digital currency, is a well-known example of a blockchain implementation that uses a consensus method to affirm, confirm, and submit a transaction to transfer value in bitcoin. A blockchain is formed while a transaction is initiated its miles broadcasted to the complete blockchain community in a peer-to-peer manner. The nodes in the network validate and confirm the transactions that is executed by the miners using the consensus algorithms. The established transaction may want to either a cryptocurrency or a clever settlement. The new transaction that is demonstrated can be a part of the ledger within the block. In the cease, the existing blockchain is appended with the new block, hence finishing the transaction. Blockchain technology is often claimed to be an "unhackable" generation. But 51% attacks permit hazard actors to "gain control over more than half of a blockchain's compute electricity and corrupt the integrity of the shared ledger. While this particular attack is expensive and hard, the reality is that it has become an effective way that protection professionals need to treat blockchain as a beneficial technology. The 51% attack exploits what is known as the 51% problem: "If a single party owns 51% of a mining pool, it is possible to falsify access to the blockchain, taking into account double spending, or even fork a new chain to the benefit of the mining pool."

"Blockchain reduces trust from a single source and distributes it among all nodes in the network. Advanced features of blockchain include immutability, which means records cannot be edited or deleted. But 51% attacks permit hazard actors to corrupt the integrity of the shared ledger"

For the future generation of virtual financial systems, we believe the hard and fast blockchain design principles may be utilized to create software programmes and services, as well as to re-imagine business models and even entire countries. This module frames the blockchain revolution's seven design standards.

1. Stability of the network

2. Power Distribution

3. Use of Value as an Incentive

4. Security

5. Privacy

6. Rights are protected

7. Inclusion

1.2 Characteristics of Blockchain Technology

The five most important characteristics of blockchain technology.

a) **P2P Network:** Blockchain technology is a peer-to-peer network in which existing devices can participate and eventually become part of the network. The P2P network also enables computer systems across a network to collaborate and provide combined processing power to the entire network.

b) **Cryptographic Hash Function:** Another key feature of blockchain technology is the use of a new cryptographic hash feature. The hash function takes an enter after which outputs a value that is then related to the next hash function. It is a one-way feature that makes it impossible for hackers to wager the value. It protects the information in a very viable way. Also, the hash function works for legitimate users who personalize the records or assets.

c) **Distributed Ledgers:** The distributed ledger function is one of the first-class features of blockchain. It allows peers to have a copy of the ledger. To make sure that they do not have to download the whole database, advanced strategies are used to make sure consensus is maintained within the network. It additionally enables peers to validate records quickly without the need to depend on a centralized authority. Furthermore, it ensures that no fraud occurs in the surrounding area.

d) **Pseudonymity:** The blockchain network additionally enables users to stay anonymous if they need to.

e) **Immutability:** Lastly, the cryptographic hash function, distributed ledger, and other functions make sure that the statistics, as soon as stored, can't be changed without the unique consumer's permission. The five key characteristics of blockchain technology define blockchain technology the most.

1.3 Advantages of Blockchain Technology

Blockchain's distinct properties provide solutions to a wide range of business problems. Here are some of the most significant advantages of blockchain technology, as well as instances of sectors that are taking advantage of them.

a) Decentralized structure:

Decentralization isn't a new idea at all. When making a technological arrangement, there are three main types of network structures that come to mind: centralized, decentralized, and distributed. While blockchain technologies frequently utilize decentralized networks, which is the focal area of blockchain technology, their strength is that no additional instance is necessary to authenticate transactions or activities, significantly lowering transaction validation times. In other words, decentralization is defined as the transfer of control and decision-making from a centralized entity (person, organization, or group thereof) to a dispersed network in the context of blockchain technology.

"In the context of blockchain technology, decentralisation refers to the transfer of control and decision-making from a centralised entity (a person, an organisation, or a group thereof) to a distributed network. Because no additional instance is required to validate transactions or activities, transaction validation durations are reduced by a factor of several orders of magnitude".

b) Trust:

Every business connection is built on the foundation of trust. It is the foundation of success, and it is an important aspect of how we care for our business networks. We also use intermediates in our connections, and they are responsible for building trust and earning our confidence. Blockchain creates trust between different groups of people (connected in Byzantine manner) where trust is either nonexistent or not clear. As a result, these businesses are willing to do business with each other that might not have been possible without an intermediary. This means that they are willing to do business with each other that might not have been possible without an intermediary. The enablement of trust is one blockchain's most cited benefits. One real example is real estate. The real estate marketplace also suffers from a lack of trust. It is straightforward to commit fraud and create paperwork. To ensure trust, a large amount of paperwork must be checked and controlled by more than one entity, such as government agencies, banks, and so on. When it comes to blockchain, you no longer have to deal with so many intermediaries. It is a trustless platform. This means that you know what you're doing and what you're moving into. You can verify the proprietor of an asset before making the deal. The agreements are transparent and tamper-evidence. This makes everything work easily. It also means that you need to do little or no office work, enhancing your purchasing experience to an entirely new level. In fact, it affects the real estate markets heavily, which is related to the global economy. Therefore, blockchain can rework the global economic system.

> *"Every business connection is built on the foundation of trust. As a result, businesses are willing to do business with each other that might not have been possible without an intermediary. The enablement of trust without third party is one of the most cited benefits of using a digital ledger called a blockchain".*

c) Enhanced Security and Privacy

Blockchain has the potential to drastically alter the perception of your sensitive and critical information. Because of its design, blockchain technology creates a data structure with intrinsic security properties, which is a result of its design. Blockchain, as its name suggests, forms from a network of computers coming together to confirm a "block," making it far more secure than other record-keeping systems. A ledger then adds this block, forming a 'chain'. With the participation of users across a distributed network, blockchain technology allows for decentralization to be accomplished. There is no single point of failure, and a single user cannot make changes to the record of transactional information. Blockchain creates an unchangeable, end-to-end encrypted record that aids in preventing fraud and unauthorized activity. Blockchain handles privacy concerns by anonymizing personal data and limiting access through permissions. Because data is stored over a network of computers rather than on a single server, hackers have a tough time accessing it.

"Blockchain technology creates a data structure with intrinsic security properties. With the participation of users across a distributed network, blockchain technology allows for decentralisation. Data is stored over a network of computers rather than on a single server, hackers have a tough time accessing it".

d) Greater Transparency and Traceability

In the absence of blockchain technology, each business is required to manage its own database. Blockchain replicates transactions and data in various locations due to its distributed ledger nature. Anyone can view the transaction ledger for public addresses, which is the best feature of blockchain. All network participants with appropriate permissions see the same information concurrently, ensuring complete transparency. All transactions are irreversible, time- and date-stamped. This enables members to view the complete transaction history and essentially eliminates the possibility of fraud. Blockchain provides an audit trail during asset transfers, documenting the asset's provenance at every step of its journey. This is particularly useful in areas where users (nodes of blockchain) are worried about environmental or violation of rights or in industries where counterfeiting and fraud are a problem. Using blockchain technology, it is now possible to exchange data regarding provenance directly with customers. Traceability data can also reveal flaws in any supply chain, such as when items are left unattended on a loading dock while waiting to be transported. In short, blockchain can help with traceability by enabling whole networks, while updating to a single shared ledger enables absolute data visibility, and a single source of truth. Supply Chain Management (SCM) is a real-life example of how blockchain works seamlessly with the supply chain. Any product that you purchase desires to undergo a chain of destinations earlier than it arrives at your doorstep. During its journey time, it can be open to a couple of fraud entities that could tamper with the product for their personal advantage. If that happens, you'll no longer get the product that you paid for. You might get a tampered product or a product that is absolutely changed with the aid of a fraudster. In any case, it is straightforward to capture fraud items. In fact, it's an outstanding way to provide product provenance and ensure that the purchasers are getting the genuine product they are buying. Blockchain utilization in the supply chain solves all of these issues. By using blockchain, corporations can preserve a complete record of the situation of the product. If the product is modified or tampered with, the gadget will get alerted and hence discard it from the supply chain. In the end, one will get a genuine product in their hand.

 *"Blockchain enables networks to directly share provenance data with customers. Transactions are irrevocable and time-stamped, preventing fraud. Traceability data can expose tampered transactions".*

e) Higher Efficiency and Speed

Blockchain transactions can be executed significantly quicker than conventional methods, as they eliminate the need for intermediaries and manual processes. In certain cases, blockchain can finalize a transaction in just a few seconds or even quicker. However, timings can vary; the speed at which a blockchain-based system processes transactions depends on various factors, including the size of each block of data and the level of network traffic. When it comes to the speed of processing, blockchain technology has been found to frequently surpass more conventional processes and technologies. Through the utilization of blockchain technology, Walmart was able to track down the origin of mango slices rapidly and efficiently in a moment. The completion of transactions is a time constraint that is required by many providers of payment facilitation services.

If you need to transfer funds quickly for an emergency, this could be an issue. When sending money from abroad, the process takes much longer. Before transferring funds via the SWIFT messaging system, banks usually hold payments for a few days. Banks are used for this purpose because of the strict regulations surrounding international money transfers. On the other hand, the waiting period will be lengthened by the additional intermediaries. The answer is provided via the blockchain. The recipient will not have to wait many days to receive the cash when you transfer funds. Banks and other financial organizations are eager to use digital tokens for large-scale money transfers. In most cases, it makes banking and financial institution transactions faster and safer. Many believe that the advent of the blockchain era will drastically improve the speed of financial transactions.

"Transactions can be completed in a fraction of the time using this technology, and documents can be stored on the same chain as the transactions themselves eliminating the need to exchange paper".

f) Increase Business Efficiency

Blockchain technology offers new business models, eliminates intermediary costs and time, and builds trust among actors in an ecosystem. Blockchain additionally offers you extra probabilities to earn. *Good* companies are slowly embracing blockchain and assisting connect humans as this technology can boom their enterprise performance. Blockchain is facilitating in the transformation of businesses in a variety of industries around the world. Through the elimination of duplication of work, better trust leads to greater efficiency. Blockchain is transforming industries as diverse as supply chain management, food delivery, financial services, government, retail, Better Healthcare System, and others.

1.4 History and Evolution of Blockchain

It is vital to know about the history of blockchain for both blockchain enthusiasts and blockchain aspirants. So, in order to help our readers, understand the blockchain history and evolution, we have put together a detailed guide to the history of blockchain technology with its detailed evolution.

1.4.1 Early Years of Blockchain Technology: 1991-2008

The blockchain technology was described in 1991 by way of studies by scientists Stuart Haber and W. Scott Stornetta. They desired to introduce a computationally practical solution for time-stamping virtual documents in order that they could not be backdated or tampered with. They broaden a machine using the concept of a cryptographically secured chain of blocks to keep the time-stamped files.

In 1992, Merkle Trees were integrated into the layout, which makes the blockchain extra efficient by way of permitting several files to be gathered into one block. Merkle Trees are used to create a "secured chain of blocks". It stored a series of data points, and every piece of statistical data was linked to the one before it. The most modern file in this chain carries the history of the complete chain. However, this generation went unused, and the patent lapsed in 2004.

"Blockchain technology was first described in 1991 by Stuart Haber and W. Scott Stornetta. Merkle Trees provide a "secured block chain". The most recent file in this chain contains the chain's history."

In 2004, computer scientist and cryptographic activist Hal Finney introduced a gadget known as Reusable Proof of Work (RPoW) as a prototype for virtual cash. It became a huge early step in the history of cryptocurrencies. The RPoW device worked by receiving a non-exchangeable or non-fungible Hash cash-based evidence of labour token in exchange, resulting in an RSA-signed token that will be transferred from character to character. RPoW solved the double-spending problem by keeping the ownership of tokens registered on a dependent-on server. This server was designed to allow customers in any part of the world to confirm its correctness and integrity in real-time.

Furthermore, in 2008, Satoshi Nakamoto conceptualised the idea of distributed blockchains. He improves the layout in a unique manner to add blocks to the initial chain without requiring them to be signed via trusted events. The modified trees might include a relaxed history of data exchanges. It utilises a peer-to-peer community for timestamping and verifying every change. It may be managed autonomously without requiring a central authority. These improvements have been so beneficial that they make blockchains the spine of cryptocurrencies. Today, the design serves as the general public ledger for all transactions inside the cryptocurrency space.

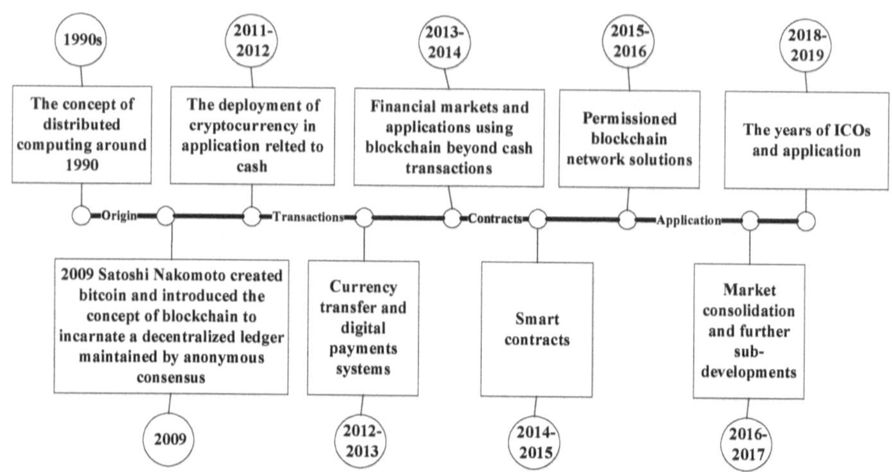

Figure 1.2: Blockchain Technology Growth

"In 2004, Hal Finney introduced a gadget known as Reusable Proof of Work (RPoW) as a prototype for virtual cash. Satoshi Nakamoto conceptualised the idea of distributed blockchains in 2008. Today, the design serves as the general public ledger for all transactions inside the cryptocurrency space."

1.4.2 Blockchain 1.0-Bitcoin Emergence: 2008-2013

The majority of people believe that Bitcoin and Blockchain are the same thing. However, that isn't always the case, as one is the underlying technology that powers most programs, which certainly one of them is cryptocurrencies.

Bitcoin came into being in 2008 as the first application of Blockchain technology. Satoshi Nakamoto, in his whitepaper, described it as a digital peer-to-peer device. Nakamoto fashioned the genesis block, from which different blocks have been mined, interconnected, resulting in one of the biggest chains of blocks ever, each wearing one-of-a-kind portions of statistics and transactions. Ever since Bitcoin, a utility of blockchain, hit the airwaves, some programmes have cropped up, all of which seek to leverage the ideas and competencies of the virtual ledger technology. Consequently, the history of the blockchain includes a long list of programmes that have been created over time.

The evolution of blockchain technology has been steady and promising. The words "block" and "chain" have been used one at a time in Satoshi Nakamoto's unique paper, but have been sooner or later popularised as a unmarried phrase, "the Blockchain," via 2016. In recent times, the document length of the cryptocurrency blockchain containing records of all transactions that took place in the community has grown from 20 GB to a hundred GB.

"Bitcoin came into being in 2008 as the first application of Bitcoin technology. Satoshi Nakamoto fashioned the genesis block, from which different blocks have been mined, interconnected. In recent times, the document length of the cryptocurrency blockchain has grown from 20 GB to a hundred GB."

1.4.3 Blockchain 2.0-Ethereum Development: 2013-2015

As one of the first contributors to the Bitcoin codebase, Vitalik Buterin is among a growing list of builders who feel Bitcoin has not yet reached its full potential when it comes to leveraging the entire competencies of the blockchain era. Concerned by Bitcoin's obstacles, Buterin began working on what he felt would be a malleable blockchain which could carry out various capabilities in addition to being a peer-to-peer network. A brand new public blockchain was launched in 2013 with enhanced functionalities compared to Bitcoin, a development that has proven to be a watershed moment in blockchain history. Buterin differentiated Ethereum from the Bitcoin Blockchain by way of allowing a characteristic that lets human beings file different belongings together with slogans as well as contracts. The new function multiplied Ethereum's functionalities from being a cryptocurrency to being a platform for growing decentralized programmes as well.

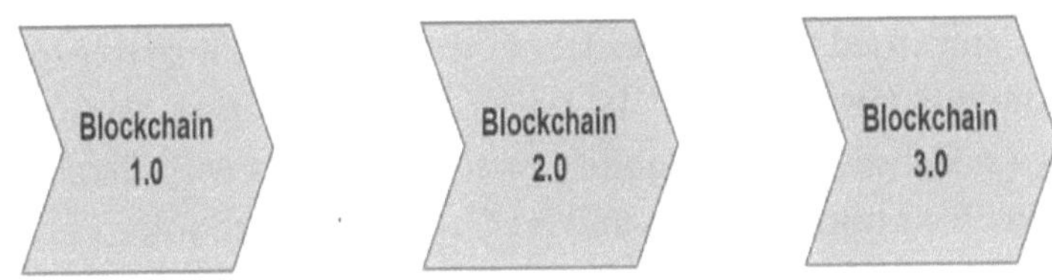

Figure 1.3: Blockchain Expansion

Officially launched in 2015, the Ethereum blockchain has developed to be one of the largest programmes of its generation given its ability to guide clever contracts used to carry out various capabilities. The Ethereum blockchain platform has additionally succeeded in amassing an active developer network that has established a true atmosphere. The Ethereum blockchain processes the largest range of daily transactions thanks to its potential to support clever contracts and decentralised packages. Its market cap has also increased appreciably in the cryptocurrency space.

"Bitcoin came into being in 2008 as the first application of Bitcoin technology. Satoshi Nakamoto fashioned the genesis block, from which different blocks have been mined, interconnected. In recent times, the document length of the cryptocurrency blockchain has grown from 20 GB to a hundred GB."

1.4.4 Blockchain 3.0: 2018

The history and progress of blockchain encompass more than merely Ethereum and Bitcoin. In recent years, various projects have emerged, all utilizing the capabilities of blockchain technology. New initiatives have aimed to address several shortcomings of Bitcoin and Ethereum, while also introducing new functionalities that utilize blockchain capabilities.

Among the new blockchain packages is NEO, promoted as the first open-source, decentralized blockchain platform launched in China. Even with the United States' ban on cryptocurrencies, the realm of blockchain technology continues to thrive. NEO casts itself as the Chinese Ethereum, having already acquired the backing of Alibaba CEO Jack Ma, as it plots to have the same effect as Baidu in the U.S. In the race to accelerate the improvement of the Internet of Things, a few builders got it in shape, to leverage the blockchain era and came up with IOTA. The cryptocurrency platform is optimised for the Internet of factors because it strives to provide zero transaction costs as well as particular verification tactics. It also addresses a number of the scalability issues associated with Blockchain 1.0 and Bitcoin. In addition to IOTA and NEO, other 2d-technology blockchain structures are also having a ripple impact within the area. The Monero, Zcash, and Dash blockchains were created to address some of the security and scalability issues associated with early blockchain applications. Dubbed as "privacy altcoins," the three blockchain platforms are seeking to offer excessive levels of privacy and protection when it comes to transactions.

The blockchain history discussed above involves public blockchain networks, whereby anybody can get right of entry to the contents of a network. However, as generation has evolved, a number of agencies have begun to adopt generation internally as a means of improving operational efficiency. Large corporations are spending a lot of money to hire experts in order to get a head start on using this generation. Companies like Microsoft, KPMG, and IBM seem to be leading the way when it comes to looking into how blockchains can be used. This has led to what are now called personal, hybrid, and federated blockchains.

"In the last few years, there have been a lot of projects that use blockchain technology. New projects have tried to fix some of the flaws in Bitcoin and Ethereum, like how hard it is to send money. They are spending a lot of money to hire experts so they can start using this generation early."

1.4.5 Future of Blockchain: 2020

The future of the blockchain generation seems vivid, in part, due to the manner in which governments and businesses are making an investment, as they are trying to find ways to spur innovations and packages. It is turning into an increasingly cleaner and safer world that sooner or later there might be a public blockchain that absolutely everyone can use. Advocates expect the generation to assist in the automation of maximum duties currently treated by specialists in all sectors. The era is already finding wonderful use in delivering control, in addition to inside the cloud computing commercial enterprise. In the future, the technology must also find its way into commonplace items such as search engines on the internet.

As the era evolves, Gartner Trend Insights expects at least one enterprise built on blockchain to return to being worth more than $10 billion by 2022. Due to the Blockchain Digital Transformation, the research company expects the enterprise price to increase to over $176 billion by 2025 and exceed $3.1 trillion by 2030.

> *"Blockchain is becoming a cleaner and safer world. Supporters hope that the next generation will help with the automation of most jobs. Technology must also be used in things like search engines on the internet in the future, so that it can be used in everyday things. It's expected that at least one business built on blockchain will be worth more than $10 billion by 2022."*

1.5 Blockchain Implementation Environment

1.5.1 Ethereum: 2013

The concept of Ethereum was developed by programmer Vitalik Buterin in 2013. In addition to the original founders of Ethereum, Gavin Wood, Charles Hoskinson, Anthony Di Iorio, and Joseph Lubin also played significant roles in its creation. Ethereum is a decentralised blockchain platform that facilitates the establishment of a peer-to-peer network for the safe execution and verification of application code, commonly referred to as smart contracts. Smart contracts enable participants to engage in transactions with one another in a decentralised manner, eliminating the need for a central authority that is trusted by all parties involved. The Ethereum protocol is not under the ownership or control of any individual, yet it needs decision-making processes to effectively adopt changes that promote the network's sustainability and success.

1.5.2 Hyperledger: 2015

In 2015, the Linux Foundation unveiled an umbrella mission for open supply blockchain. They went on to call it Hyperledger, which till date acts as a collaborative improvement of allotted ledgers. Under the leadership of Brian Behlendorf, Hyperledger seeks to enhance go-enterprise collaboration for the development of blockchain and disbursed ledgers. Hyperledger makes a speciality of encouraging the use of the blockchain era to improve the performance and reliability of modern-day systems to help global enterprise transactions.

1.5.3 EOS.IO: 2017

EOS is the brainchild of a private organisation block. One came into being in 2017, with the publication of a white paper detailing a new blockchain protocol powered by EOS, the local cryptocurrency. Unlike different blockchain protocols, EOS tries to emulate attributes of real computer systems, including the CPU and GPU. For that purpose, EOS.IO doubles up as a clever settlement platform, in addition to a decentralised working gadget. Its foremost purpose is to encourage the deployment of decentralised packages via an independent, decentralised enterprise.

1.5.4 Algorand Blockchain(ABC): 2019

Algorand was founded in 2019 by Silvio Micali, who is a professor of computer science at the Massachusetts Institute of Technology. In 2017, Silvio launched Algorand with the main objective of overseeing important research projects in the fields of theory, security, and crypto finance. Algorand is a network that operates autonomously and in a decentralised manner, utilising blockchain technology. The platform provides a diverse selection of secure, efficient, and scalable applications. Algorand's technology offers a range of high-performance layer 1 blockchains that provide security, scalability, privacy, and transaction finality. A layer-1 blockchain refers to a set of solutions that enhance the underlying protocol in order to enhance the scalability of the system.

1.6 Various Definitions of Blockchain

There are various definitions of blockchain; it depends on how you examine it. If you examine it from a business perspective it could be described in that context, in case you study it from a technical perspective one can outline it in view of that.

1   The heart of Blockchain is a peer-to-peer distributed ledger that is cryptographically comfortable, append-most effective, immutable, and updateable most effectively through peer consensus.

2   In terms of business perspectives, a blockchain is certainly a ramification of transactions bundled collectively in order to organize them logically. A connection with a previous block is likewise protected inside the block unless it is a genesis block. A "genesis block" is the primary block inside the blockchain.

3   According to enterprise strategies, a blockchain may be defined as a platform whereby peers can exchange values through the use of

transactions without the need for a primary arbitrator. This is a powerful concept in realizing the ability of blockchain technology.

4 From a technical perspective, blockchain can be described as a fact shape that holds transactional information whilst ensuring protection, transparency, and decentralization. You can also think of it as a sequence of data stored in the form of blocks which might be managed by means of no single authority.

5 A blockchain is a distributed ledger that is completely open to any and all of us in the community. Once statistics are saved on a blockchain, it is extremely tough to exchange or modify them due to the fact that every transaction on a blockchain is secured with a digital signature that proves its authenticity. Due to the use of encryption and virtual signatures, the facts saved under the block on the blockchain are tamper-proof and can't be changed.

6 A blockchain is a fact shape; it is basically a linked list that uses hash recommendations in place of everyday pointers. Hash suggestions are used to point to the preceding block.

7 The blockchain is a distributed database of statistics about all transactions or digital events that have been completed and shared among collaborating parties. Each transaction is tested by most of the participants in the machine.

8 The only shape of the blockchain acts as a part of, replicated, and brought database in which admission to the document is shared, but verification is carried out through all or some of the participants. The foundation of blockchain is based on a rundown of statistics, referred to as "blocks," which can be connected to the use of cryptography to offer security.

9 A blockchain is a growing list of statistics, known as blocks, that are connected through the usage of cryptography. Each block includes a cryptographic hash of the previous block, a timestamp, and transaction statistics (commonly represented as a Merkle tree).

10 A blockchain is, in the simplest of terms, a time-stamped collection of immutable reports of facts that is controlled by a cluster of computers

no longer owned with the aid of any unmarried entity. Each of these blocks of facts (i.e., blocks) is secure and certain to each other thanks to the use of cryptographic principles. era is every so often represented as a long DNA chain, periodically growing in size when facts associated with new transactions are delivered.

 *Blockchain is a peer-to-peer distributed ledger that is cryptographically comfortable, append-most effective, immutable, and no updateable. Every transaction on a blockchain is secured with a digital signature that proves its authenticity. Due to the use of encryption and virtual signatures, the facts saved under the block on the blockchain are tamper-proof and can't be changed. Blockchain is a distributed database of statistics about all transactions or digital events. Each transaction is tested by most of the participants in the machine. Each block includes a cryptographic hash of the previous block, a timestamp, and transaction statistics (commonly represented as a Merkle tree).*

1.7 Why It's Called "Blockchain"

A blockchain is an incredibly new kind of database that has emerged as the trendy answer to storing virtual facts more securely. According to the International Data Corporation, corporations and governments will spend $2.1 billion on blockchains in 2018, more than doubling what was spent in the previous year.

The first blockchain became the database on which each Bitcoin transaction was stored. Since Bitcoin began in 2009, the blockchain has come to preserve over one hundred sixty gigabytes well worth of information approximately every time a Bitcoin is sent between two virtual wallets.

In the authentic documents describing Bitcoin, the virtual currency's new database is not called a blockchain. But it got that name over time due to the fact that all the transactions coming into the community were grouped into blocks of data and then chained collectively through the usage of sophisticated math. It's difficult to move lower back and rewrite with the older records because of this. Academics have said that this design was around before Bitcoin, but Bitcoin made it famous.

1.8 Technological Growth in Blockchain

One of the most prominent uses of blockchain is in cryptocurrency. Digital currencies or tokens, like Bitcoin, Ethereum, and Litecoin, are used for buying goods and services. Similar to the digital form of money, cryptocurrency can be used for various transactions, including dining and real estate purchases. Unlike cash, cryptocurrency utilizes blockchain technology to serve as a public ledger and a sophisticated cryptographic security system, guaranteeing that online transactions are continuously recorded and protected.

As of today, there are approximately 6,700 cryptocurrencies worldwide, with a total market capitalization of around $1.6 trillion. Bitcoin holds the majority of this value, with a single Bitcoin currently valued at $60,000. Cryptocurrencies have gained significant popularity in recent years. Here are some key reasons why they are now attracting widespread attention:

a) The security of blockchain significantly complicates theft, given that each cryptocurrency possesses a distinct, verifiable identifier linked to a particular owner.

b) Cryptocurrencies eliminate the need for different national currencies and large banks. Cryptocurrency may be delivered anywhere in the world to anyone via blockchain, eliminating the need for currency exchange or central bank involvement.

c) Cryptocurrencies have the potential to make some people wealthy. Speculators have driven up the price of cryptocurrency, particularly Bitcoin, allowing some early adopters to become billionaires. Critics argue that speculators may overlook the long-term benefits of cryptocurrencies, making it unclear whether this is a truly positive development.

d) More and more large organizations are adopting the notion of blockchain-based virtual foreign money for bills. In February 2021, Tesla notably declared that it will invest $1.5 billion in Bitcoin and use it as payment for its vehicles.

Certainly, there are many valid points raised against blockchain-based digital currencies. To begin with, the cryptocurrency market lacks full regulation. Numerous governments have swiftly embraced cryptocurrency, yet only a handful possess a solid framework of established regulations governing it. Moreover, the volatility of crypto can be attributed to the influence of speculators. In 2016, the price of Bitcoin was approximately

$450, based on the token's value. It subsequently surged to approximately $16,000 per token in 2018, fell to about $3,100, and has now ascended to over $60,000.

1.8.1 Beyond Bitcoin: Ethereum Blockchain

In the beginning, blockchain technology was built to serve as the underlying ledger system for Bitcoin. Since then, it has been closely associated with cryptocurrencies. Nevertheless, the fact that it is both transparent and secure has resulted in its widespread acceptance across a variety of industries, a significant portion of which can be ascribed to developments in the Ethereum blockchain.

In late 2013, Russian-Canadian developer Vitalik Buterin published a white paper that introduced a platform merging traditional blockchain functionalities with a significant advancement: the capacity to execute computer code. This resulted in the establishment of the Ethereum Project. The question then emerged: could Ethereum developers create sophisticated applications that would interact seamlessly on the blockchain?

"Blockchain technology has long been linked to bitcoin. Rising need for the technology's openness and security in 2013, Vitalik Buterin published a white paper proposing a blockchain platform with one major difference: computer code execution. So began the Ethereum Project."

1.9 Tokens

Ethereum developers have the capability to create tokens that represent various types of digital assets, monitor their ownership, and perform functions based on a specific set of programming rules. These tokens are applicable for managing documents, contracts, concert tickets, or even medical records. Recently, non-fungible tokens (NFTs) have surged in popularity. NFTs are distinct tokens based on blockchain technology that encapsulate digital media, including videos, music, or art. Every NFT serves to confirm the authenticity, ownership history, and exclusive rights associated with a piece of digital content. A new generation of digital creators is provided with the chance to buy, sell, and profit from their work, all while ensuring they receive proper credit and a fair share of earnings.

The potential of blockchain technology has broadened with emerging applications, influencing various sectors such as media, government, and identity security. Numerous organizations are currently investigating and creating products and ecosystems that depend significantly on this swiftly advancing technology.

Blockchain is transforming the existing landscape of innovation, allowing organizations to investigate groundbreaking ideas like peer-to-peer energy distribution and decentralized information platforms. The adaptability of technology defines it, and similarly, the applications of blockchain will evolve alongside ongoing technological advancements.

Test your skills

1. What does P2P stand for?

a) Password to Password

b) Peer to Peer

c) Product to Product

d) Private Key to Public Key

2. Who created Bitcoin?

a) Satoshi Nakamoto

b) Samsung

c) John Mcafee

d) China

3. What is a blockchain?

a) A distributed ledger on a peer to peer network

b) A type of cryptocurrency

c) An exchange

d) A centralized ledger

4.   Technically, the Blockchain and Bitcoin are the same

a)   True

b)   False

Descriptive Questions:

1)   Define Blockchain.

2)   What is a Genesis Block?

3)   List of Top Blockchain Features.

4)   Discuss the various Blockchain Implementation environment.

5)   What is Blockchain? Why It's Called "Blockchain?

6)   Explain the Historical Evolution of Blockchain Technology.

7)   What is NFT?

8)   Discuss the various Characteristics of Blockchain Technology.

9)   Write the Advantages of Blockchain Technology.

10) Difference Between Blockchain and Bitcoin?

CHAPTER – 2

ELEMENTS AND TERMS OF A BLOCKCHAIN

As we already discussed in chapter 1, A "blockchain" is a decentralised, distributed ledger that stores the history of a digital asset. By design, the data on a blockchain can't be changed, which makes it a real threat to industries like payments, cybersecurity, and healthcare. This chapter will help you to understand the basic terminology and elements of blockchain technology.

2.1 Generic Elements of a Blockchain

Although there are various types of blockchains, they all share key characteristics: they function as peer-to-peer distributed ledgers that are cryptographically secure, append-only, and immutable (meaning they are extremely difficult to edit). Changes can only occur with mutual permission or understanding among those involved. This layer of a distributed peer-to-peer network can be thought of as a layer of the Internet going for a walk on the top of the Internet, as shown in figure 2.1. If you were to walk on top of TCP/IP, it would be like SMTP, HTTP, or FTP going for walks.

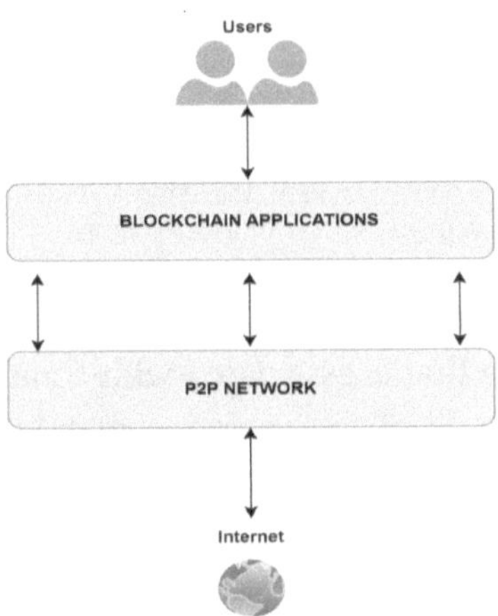

Figure 2.1: The Network View of Blockchain

Blockchain may be viewed as a platform that allows peers to exchange value through transactions without the requirement for a trusted third-party intermediary. This is how blockchain can be viewed from a commercial viewpoint. As soon as this idea is grasped, the enormous potential of blockchain technology becomes readily apparent. Because of this, a decentralized consensus system is made possible, in which the database is neither controlled nor supervised by a single authority. A blockchain is fundamentally a peer-to-peer distributed ledger that is cryptographically secure, append-only, immutable, and can only be modified through consent among participants. It can be perceived as a layer of a distributed peer-to-peer network functioning over the Internet, analogous to how protocols such as SMTP, HTTP, or FTP operate over TCP/IP, as shown in Figure 2.1.

The term "blockchain" describes the storage of data, including transactions, in the form of blocks. All nodes in the network can view these blocks, but they remain unalterable. Interference with a block's contents alters its hash value, isolating the block from the network. On average, every node in the blockchain network receives the latest version of the blockchain within 12.6 seconds. Below are some of the key characteristics commonly associated with a blockchain network.

2.1.1 Block

A blockchain is a series of sequentially arranged blocks that record information about transactions within the blockchain network. Each block is linked to the previous one, resembling a linked list in data structures. Every block contains data, and the organization of this data is determined by the particular blockchain and its method of handling information. Every block features a unique header, and the hash of its block header serves to distinctly identify each block.

Blocks perform the function of efficient virtual containers that permanently store data that is associated with transactions that take place on the chain. Some or all of the most recent transactions that were not included in earlier blocks are included in a block once it is created. As a result, we are able to draw parallels between a block and a page in a ledger or file book. Once a block is "closed," it allows the next block to be added to the blockchain. Any data recorded becomes a permanent, unalterable record, as it cannot be changed or removed.

A block is basically a collection of transactions that have been logically grouped together. It is constructed from transactions and varies in length according to the kind and structure of the blockchain in use. A reference to a preceding block is also contained within the block until it becomes a genesis block. A genesis block is the initial block in a blockchain that was hardcoded when the blockchain was created. It also depends on the type and design of a blockchain, but there are a lot of important things about a block that make it work, like the block header, hints to previous blocks and other things like the time stamp and nonce. Figure 2.2 shows these things.

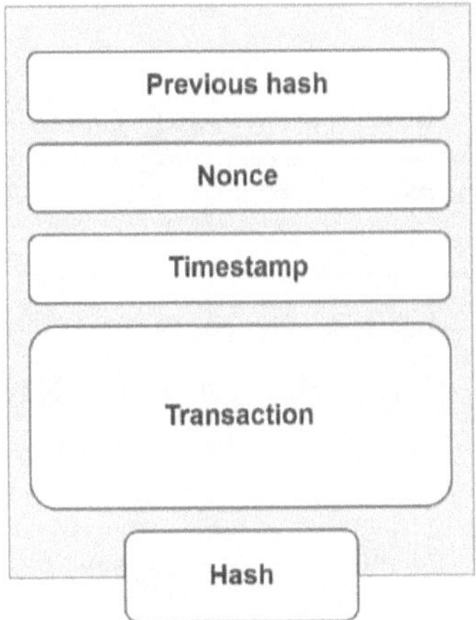

Figure 2.2: Structure of a Single Block in Blockchain

Each block has a hash, which is an essential piece of information that is contained within it. We make use of the hash to verify the legitimacy of the block and determine whether or not to include it in the chain that is currently in progress. Because each block has a unique hash, it is impossible for any malevolent actor to copy it as shown in Figure 2.3. Additionally, it serves as a gateway to access information about the block's contents, enhancing the security of that information A warning will be generated in the event that the data contained within the block is attempted to be altered. This will prohibit other blocks from accepting the block in question. The data, a hash, and the hash of the block that came before it allow us to break down the structure of each block into three distinct components.

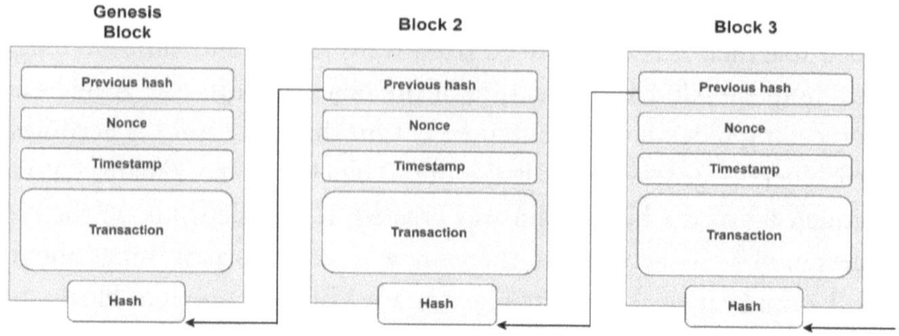

Figure 2.3: Chain of Blocks in Blockchain

A block is basically a collection of transactions that have been logically grouped together. A reference to a preceding block is also contained within the block until it becomes a genesis block. Each block has a unique header, and for my part, each such block is recognised by its block header hash.

Take, for example, the bitcoin blockchain. A block in the bitcoin blockchain carries simple information about a transaction, such as the receiver, the sender, and the quantity of bitcoin transferred.

Rather than requiring a substantial amount of storage space, a block is used to store records, which are collections of data that differ from one another. Blocks typically include the following components, though the details may vary depending on the type of blockchain:

a) **Block size:** The block size is a parameter that determines the maximum amount of data that may be stored within the block. It also defines the size limit of the block limit.

b) **Block header:** Includes details regarding the block.

c) **Transaction counter:** A number that corresponds to the total number of transactions that have been saved in the block.

d) **Transactions:** A listing of all of the transactions inside a block.

The transaction element is the most significant as it holds the greatest amount of information. The storage length indicated by the block header reflects its size, which includes the following sub-elements:

e) **Version:** It is the specific cryptocurrency protocol that is currently being utilized.

f) **Previous block hash:** The previous block's hash contains a hash of the header from the block that preceded it (in encrypted form).

g) **Hash Merkle root:** The hash of the transactions that are contained within the Merkle tree of the current block is referred to as the Hash Merkle root.

h) **Time:** A timestamp to region the block inside the blockchain.

i) **Bits:** This is the difficulty target of the hash, which indicates how challenging it is to solve the nonce.

j) **Nonce:** The encrypted value that a miner needs to decode in order to validate and close the block at the end of the mining process.

A nonce is a 32-bit field in the header that the mining program use to generate random numbers within the hash. Upon successful validation of a nonce, the hash is determined by either guessing the nonce or choosing a number that is less than it. The network subsequently finalizes the block, generates a new one with a header, and the cycle resumes.

2.1.2 Genesis Block

The genesis block represents the initial block in any blockchain protocol. The term "blockchain" is used to describe the foundation upon which new blocks are added to form a chain of blocks. This block is referenced in Block 0 from time to time. Each block in a blockchain maintains a link to the preceding block. Regarding the Genesis Block, it is possible that there is no preceding block for comparison. Technically, this indicates that the Genesis Block's "previous hash" value is established at 0. This methodology ensures that no records are processed prior to the Genesis Block. All subsequent blocks may possess sequential numbers commencing with 1 and will have a "preceding hash" assigned to the hash of the preceding block.

The hash of the genesis block is incorporated into all subsequent transactions within a newly created block. This aggregate is utilized to generate its exact hash. This process is reiterated until all new blocks are transmitted to the blockchain. The range utilized to reference the arrangement of blocks is termed the block top variety. It starts at zero with the Genesis Block.

The Genesis block is the first block in any blockchain-based protocol. Every block stores a connection with the previous block. The hash of the genesis block is added to all new transactions in a next block. This aggregate is used to create each transaction's precise hash.

The Genesis Block of Bitcoin serves as the foundational example of a proof-of-work blockchain mechanism and acts as the model for all subsequent blocks within its blockchain. In 2009, the pseudonymous developer of Bitcoin, Satoshi Nakamoto, created the Genesis Block, marking the beginning of the ongoing cryptocurrency explosion.

2.1.3 Addresses

Addresses are unique identifiers used in blockchain transactions to distinguish between senders and recipients. Typically, an address is generated from a public key. Addresses can be reused by the same user, but each is unique. In practice, users should avoid reusing the same address and instead establish a new one for each transaction. This newly established address remains unique. As a best practice, users should create a different address for each transaction to prevent being associated with a single identity, so safeguarding their anonymity. In layman's terms, a blockchain address is a destination for blockchain transactions, similar to a URL.

2.1.4 Transaction

A transaction is the term used to describe the process by which one peer sends data to another peer. Without transactions, there would be no reason for the blockchain to exist, and this is a key component of any blockchain. Without transactions, the blockchain would be irrelevant.

A transaction's records comprise the sender, receiver, and amount. This technique is very similar to a modern credit card transaction, with the primary distinction being that it does not involve a centralized authority. For example, when an end user transmits Cryptocurrency to someone else, the transaction causes a change in the blockchain's agreed-upon state. Since the blockchain is a decentralized network, all nodes must be updated. Each node keeps an identical copy of the ledger, which contributes to the overall state of the blockchain.

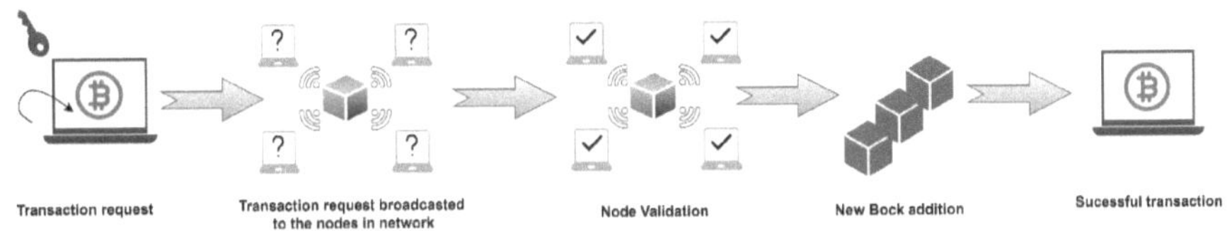

Figure 2.4: Transaction Process in Blockchain

As mentioned in figure 2.4 transactions are bundled and brought to each node inside the shape of a block. As new transactions are dispensed throughout the community, they're independently established and "processed" by each node. This steady motion of coin is what constitutes the facts inside any blockchain structure, whilst the ways wherein transactions are treated and verified varies by using implementation.

> *The sender, receiver, and price are all part of a transaction's records. A nation trade can be triggered by a single transaction. Each transaction starts a chain with an agreed-upon state that is modified by the transaction.*

2.2 Scripting or Programming Language

A number of computer languages, including C++, Java, C#, JavaScript, Go, Python, Ruby, and Solidity, are considered to be among the most popular choices for the construction of blockchain smart contracts. While the other languages are well-established and frequently used, Solidity is the only novel language that was built particularly for the purpose of constructing smart contracts that are based on Ethereum protocol. The following programming languages are related with a few of the most prominent blockchain platforms. These languages also include languages that can be utilized to construct blockchain applications that are compatible with several blockchains.

Blockchain	Written In	Language Support	Consensus
ARK	JavaScript	JavaScript, Go, Python, C#, TypeScript, Kotlin, Ruby, Swift, PHP	DPoS
CORDA	Kotlin	Java, Kotlin,	

Blockchain	Written In	Language Support	Consensus
ETHEREUM	Go, C++, Rust	Solidity	PoW/PoS
EOS	C++	WebAssembly, C, C++	DPoS
HYPERLEDGER FABRIC	Go, Java, JavaScript, Python	Go, Java, Kotlin	
LISK	JavaScript, Node.js	JavaScript	DPoS
NEO	C#	C#, Java, Kotlin, Python	PoS
QTUM	C++, Python, TypeScript	C++, Python, Rust, Go, Lua	PoS
STRATIS	C++, C#	C#	PoS
WAVES	Scala	Scala	DPoS

i) C++

The fourth most widely used programming language is C++. C++ is the language of choice for the majority of blockchain projects. Bitcoin, Ripple, Litecoin, Monero, EOS, Stellar, and QTUM are some of the most popular C++-based blockchains.

ii) C#

Microsoft's C# is the 7th most widely used open source programming language. 5 to 8 million C# and.NET developers are employed worldwide. Stratis, NEO, and IOTA are just a few of the popular blockchains that make use of C#.

iii) GO

An entirely new language, Golang, has been developed by Google and is becoming increasingly popular. Ethereum, Dero, Hyperledger Fabric, and GoChain are just a few of the blockchains built with GO.

iv) JAVA

The most common programming language is Java. Ethereum, IOTA, NEM, Hyperledger Fabric, and NEO are examples of well-known blockchains constructed with Java.

v) Python

Python ranks as the second most widely used programming language in the development of blockchain technology. Among the blockchains that have been constructed using Python, some of the most well-known ones include Ethereum, Hyperledger Fabric, Steem, and NEO. Python's adaptability in blockchain programming has made it a dominant force in application development, Internet of Things app development, and network server development.

vi) Solidity

Solidity is a high-level programming language designed specifically for writing smart contracts on the Ethereum blockchain and other blockchain platforms that support Ethereum's Virtual Machine (EVM). It is influenced by JavaScript, Powershell, and C++, is the first blockchain programming language one must master. Especially if you intend to develop dApps or intend to enter the ICO development market. Solidity is a new programming language for building Ethereum smart contracts. Ethereum and its forked and inherited projects are the only blockchains developed and supported by Solidity.

Vitalik Buterin, the creator of Ethereum, created the Solidity blockchain programming language. It provides a slew of advantages to blockchain development companies, including Developer-friendliness, Infrastructure for JavaScript, debuggers, and Programming with static types, Inheritance attributes in smart contracts, and precise precision.

The most popular programming languages for blockchain development include C#, C++, Java, Python, and Go. If you want to learn about blockchain and become a blockchain developer, read How to Become a Blockchain Developer.

2.3 Virtual machine

Virtual machines are essential in the blockchain ecosystem, offering a safe and decentralized environment for the execution of smart contracts and decentralized applications (dApps). They empower developers to construct intricate applications while maintaining consistency and security throughout the network.

The EVM is an extension of transaction scripts. While a transaction script may have limitations in its execution, a virtual machine enables the execution of Turing-complete code on a blockchain through smart contracts. Not all blockchains feature virtual machines, but many, such as the Ethereum Virtual Machine (EVM) and Chain Virtual Machine (CVM), utilize them to run applications. In simple terms, a Virtual Machine (VM) functions as a computer operating on the blockchain, allowing smart contracts from various sources to interact with one another. A VM is similar to any physical computer, such as a laptop, smartphone, or server. It includes a central processing unit, memory, storage for data, and internet connectivity if needed. While the hardware components of your computer are tangible, VMs. are often regarded as virtual or software-defined computers that run on physical servers and exist solely as code.

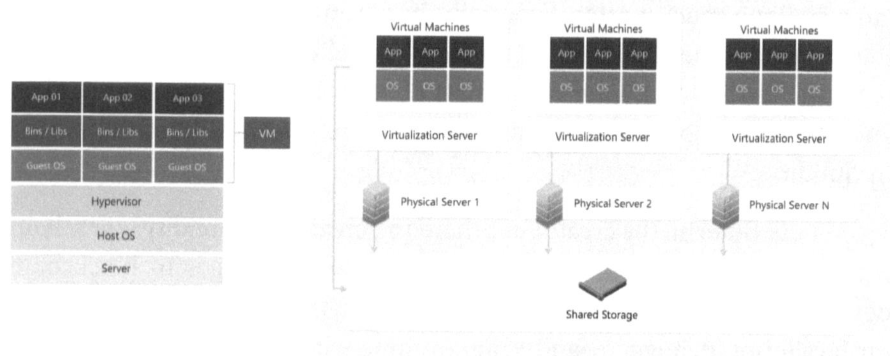

Figure 2.5: Virtualization Process

Virtualization is the process of creating a software-based, or "virtual," representation of a computer that uses allocated CPU, memory, and storage resources from a physical host computer, such as a personal computer, or a remote server, such as one located in a cloud provider's data center, as shown in figure 2.5. A virtual machine is a computer file that emulates a physical computer. This file is commonly referred to as an image. It can run as an independent computing environment within a window, typically to execute an alternative operating system or to serve as the user's complete computing experience, as is common in many people's computer usage. The virtual computer is segregated from the rest of the system. This means that applications running in a virtual machine cannot affect the host computer's principal operating system.

2.4 State machine

A blockchain can be viewed as a state transition mechanism whereby a state is modified from its initial form to the next and eventually to its final form because of a transaction execution and validation process by nodes.

2.5 Nodes

Blockchain nodes serve as the essential links within any blockchain application ecosystem, built on a foundation of peer-to-peer technology. This technology utilizes blockchain nodes to facilitate communication within blockchain networks. In an ideal scenario, blockchain nodes are created to maintain full copies of the data recorded on distributed ledgers. A node within a blockchain community exhibits various capabilities depending on its chosen position. A node has the capability to propose and validate transactions, as well as perform mining to promote consensus and stabilize the blockchain. This is accomplished through the implementation of a consensus protocol. Typically, this refers to PoW. Nodes can perform various functions, including basic charge verification (lightweight nodes), validators, and many other features based on the type of blockchain utilized and the role assigned to the node.

Nodes are the essence of blockchain technology. Blockchain nodes form a network of devices that sustain a blockchain by carrying out various tasks. A computer or phone that is connected to the internet (and has an IP address because of this) is a node.

Every node in a blockchain network maintains a copy of the ledger, has the capability to execute transactions, and can communicate the latest block transactions to and from other nodes. Every blockchain features its unique node tree, collectively forming a "distributed" ledger that maintains an accurate record of all transactions within the blockchain. Node operators get compensated for allocating computational resources to store and authenticate transactions on blockchains such as Bitcoin by earning transaction fees in the cryptocurrency of the blockchain.

Although any laptop can theoretically become a node, the computing power necessary to maintain a node and validate transactions is far beyond the capabilities of the common computer.

There are various types of nodes. The majority of blockchain nodes just connect to the network to complete basic operations.

- Lightweight: just download block headers rather than whole block ledgers, which is sufficient information to mine or validate a transaction. These are known as lightweight nodes.

- Full: A full node downloads the entire blockchain and utilizes the consensus process to validate and add new transactions to the blocks. Master nodes can facilitate other actions on a blockchain, such as voting events, conducting protocol operations, and enforcing the blockchain's rules, in addition to performing all of the functions that full nodes can. These nodes often have a lot more RAM and are always online. As a result, they require more power, maintenance, storage space, uptime, and other resources than regular nodes.

2.6 Block Mining

A peer-to-peer network process, blockchain mining, is used to confirm and verify transactions. Block mining includes blockchain miners who have submitted the transaction information to the public ledger of transactions. In the ledgers, blockchain miners keep the blocks safe and link them together so that they form a chain. A blockchain is a network of computers that contains the same history of transactions that occur over a single blockchain, with the transaction validated by every system that participates in the transaction, completely distributed across all nodes (computers) in a network. The decentralized nature of the blockchain makes it independent of any centralized or third-party control. The blockchain is secured by miners. Anyone can participate in the mining network. The miner uses his CPU or GPU to solve specific mathematical problems based on applications and broadcast on the blockchain network. Mining is the process of adding transaction records to the public ledger of the blockchain. A transaction is only valid if it is signed by the sender. The steps involved in block mining are as follows:

First: Any new transaction on the blockchain must be broadcast to the entire network.

Second: Miners must validate and verify new transactions.

Third: Every node adds the bundle to the block.

Forth: Each node must locate the proof of work for the linked block.

Fifth: After successfully finding the proof, the message was broadcast to the entire network.

Sixth: Every participating node accepts it only if it is valid.

Seventh: Working on the next block shows acceptance of proof of work.

To understand how cryptocurrency mining works, you need to know that, unlike traditional ways of making money, cryptocurrency doesn't have a central clearinghouse. Think about Bitcoin. Most Bitcoin transactions are confirmed in decentralized clearing systems, where people use their computing power to confirm the same. This way of making sure that transactions are valid could be called "mining." Using a lot of computer power is needed to mine bitcoins. Over time, the number of bitcoins that can be mined is going down. Bitcoins, according to Satoshi Nakamoto, are finite in supply. There will only ever be 21 million bitcoins created. The term "blockchain mining" is used to describe the process of adding transaction data to the bitcoin blockchain in the middle of the article. Using this approach of adding blocks to the blockchain, Bitcoin transactions are processed, and money is securely transferred. This process of blockchain mining is carried out by a global network of individuals known as "blockchain miners." In its middle, the time period 'Blockchain mining' is used to explain the process of adding transaction statistics to the bitcoin blockchain. This method of adding blocks to the blockchain is how Bitcoin transactions are processed and cash moves around securely. This procedure of blockchain mining is done by a community of humans around the world known as "blockchain miners." Anyone can apply to come and be a blockchain miner. These blockchain miners install and run a special blockchain mining software programme that permits their computers to speak securely with one another. Once a laptop installs the software, joins the community, and begins mining bitcoins, it will become what is known as a 'node." Most of these nodes communicate with each other and process transactions to add new blocks to the blockchain, which is commonly referred to as the bitcoin network. This bitcoin community runs at some stage in the day. Its systems are worth hundreds of thousands of dollars in bitcoin transactions, and since it came out in 2009, it has never been hacked or gone down.

2.6.1 Types of Mining

Mining can become complicated, and a standard computer or PC will not be able to simplify it. As a result, it necessitates an entirely unique mix of hardware and software that is tuned to the individual. It allows you to create a custom set for mining specific blocks. The mining mission is broken into three categories:

a)   Individual Mining

When mining is done through an individual, the player needs to sign up as a miner. When a transaction takes place, a math problem is given to every single user in the blockchain network to solve. The first person to clean it up gets a reward. Once the answer is found, all of the miners in the blockchain network will check that the decrypted value is correct and then add it to the blockchain. So, making sure the transaction is real.

b)   Pool Mining

In pool mining, a group of users work together to approve the transaction. Sometimes, it's hard to decrypt the encoded information on your own because the information in the blocks is so complicated. So, a group of miners works together to figure it out. After the result has been confirmed, the praise is shared among all customers.

c)   Cloud Mining

Cloud mining helps get rid of the need for hardware and software on a laptop. It's a simple way to get blocks off the ground. With cloud mining, you don't have to worry about keeping track of all your equipment, keeping track of order times, or promoting your earnings. Even though it is trouble-free, it has its own set of problems. Because of the limits on bitcoin hashing, the ability to do business is limited. Because the reward profits are low, the operating costs are going up. There aren't many ways to make software better, and there aren't many ways to check it.

2.6.2 Mining Bitcoins

Bitcoins can be traded, or they can be mined. People who mine bitcoins are given bitcoins as a reward. This system is the centre around which the Bitcoin economy turns. As the cost and difficulty of mining bitcoins on your own keeps going up, cloud-based mining services have slowly started to pop up. With these services, anyone can rent the processing power of mining equipment and mine bitcoins from anywhere in the world.

- Obtain a bitcoin wallet: Bitcoins are saved in digital wallets in an encrypted way. This will keep your bitcoins secure.

- Secure the wallet: Because there is no ownership of bitcoins, all of us who profit have access to your wallet and can use it without restriction. So, enable two-factor authentication and save the pockets on a PC that does not have Internet access or in an external tool.

- Choose a cloud mining service provider: Cloud mining carriers permit customers to lease processing or hashing power to mine bitcoins remotely. Popular cloud mining carrier vendors are Genesis Mining and Hash Flare.

- Select a cloud mining bundle: To pick a package, you'll need to determine how much you're willing to pay and keep your eyes open to the hashing electricity the package deal will provide. Cloud mining corporations will mostly envisage a Return on Investment (ROI) based totally on the modern market fee of Bitcoins.

- Pick a mining pool: This is the best chance you can get to earn bitcoins without problems. There are many mining swimming pools which charge a trifling 2% of your overall earnings. Over here, you may need to create employees, which are basically subaccounts that can be used to make your contributions to the pool.

- When you see a return on investment, you should really take your money out and put it somewhere safe.

2.6.3 Uses of Blockchain Mining

To ensure that each transaction is legitimate, blockchain mining verifies each step of it. An individual's primary goal in participating is to confirm the transactions from one computer in the network to another through a maze of computer hardware and software. To prove its authenticity, encrypted data must be decrypted. In order to decrypt data that has been encoded in blocks, you'll need a combination of computational hardware and software as well as human effort. It will take a lot of time and effort for both the computer and the human to decrypt a single encrypted code. Decryption of the data will be achieved through a combination of computational speed and human intelligence. When linked to the adjacent blocks, the transaction is verified. Hash-codes are the codes that connect the blocks in a transaction. For the decryption of the encrypted data, it is necessary that these hash codes meet specific criteria.

2.7 Transactions

A block, as previously mentioned, contains a number of transactions. The number of transactions that may be included in a block is limited. It depends on the block, the length of the transaction, and any implementation restrictions on the number of transactions that may be kept in a block. Based on the consensus technique utilized, the transaction verification is conducted by impartial nodes. Technically, each transaction will have one or more inputs and outputs. When a transaction is recorded in the blockchain, it captures important details. These details are then verified and settled within seconds across all nodes. Any verified change that is registered on one ledger is also instantly registered on all other copies of the ledger.

2.7.1 Validating Transaction

The decision to include a transaction in a public blockchain chain is made by consensus. If most "nodes" (computers in the network) agree, then this means that the transaction is legitimate. The public key is available to anyone, while the user's private key is only accessible by them. You can create a secure digital identity by using both and authenticating the user via digital signature in order to perform the desired transaction and "unlock" it. For example, bitcoin transactions take place in huge numbers every day. Cryptocurrencies operate without a central administrator, and the lack of confidence can be massive with the transactions that transpire. With each transaction, new blocks are introduced to the blockchain in the community, and the validation lies within the mining results from the blockchain miners as shown in figure 2.6.

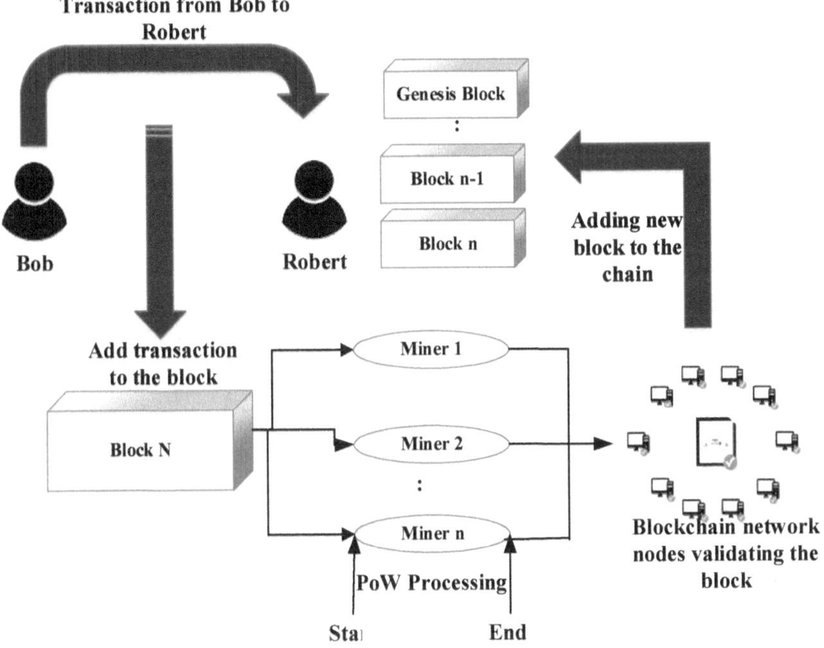

Figure 2.6: Transaction Validation Process

2.7.2 Confirming Transactions

In order to verify whether or not a transaction is real, miners use the blockchain mining method. The blockchain then contains all of the shown transactions.

2.8 Securing Network

To stabilize the transaction community, bitcoin miners work together. With more users mining the blockchain, the blockchain community's protection increases. Network protection guarantees that there are no fraudulent activities occurring with cryptocurrencies on the network.

Mining because the name suggests is connection with something this is to be bored or dug to get the excellent final results. Blockchain mining refers to the activity completed by using miners at the community to get the brand-new blocks introduced to the blockchain. In different phrases," Mining is the mechanism that lets in the blockchain to be created securely and in a decentralized manner. It provides the idea for the cryptocurrency gadget and permits a peer-to-peer community without a central authority.

Consensus is required for a transaction to be included in a public blockchain. Computational speed and human intelligence will be used to decrypt the data. While anyone can see the public key, only the user has access to the user's private key. The mechanism by which the blockchain can be created safely and decentralised is known as mining. Cryptocurrencies are decentralised, and the lack of trust in them can be enormous. Network security ensures that cryptocurrencies are not used for illicit purposes on the network.

Blockchain mining involves several critical procedures that are vital for confirming and incorporating transactions into the public ledger of the blockchain. The parties participating in this process are referred to as blockchain miners, whose primary role is to validate the movement of cash between computers inside the network, utilizing a complex array of processing hardware and software. Blockchain miners secure and connect blocks to create a chain within the ledgers.

Blockchains are named for their structural components, namely 'blocks' and 'chain.' The chain denotes the connections between adjacent neighborhood blocks. Each blockchain signifies a distinct code authentication expressly encrypted within the network software. The procedure is also gratifying. A single user does not manage the mining process; rather, multiple users compete for a collective authentication to obtain the benefits. Every successful mining operation yields a reward of several coins.

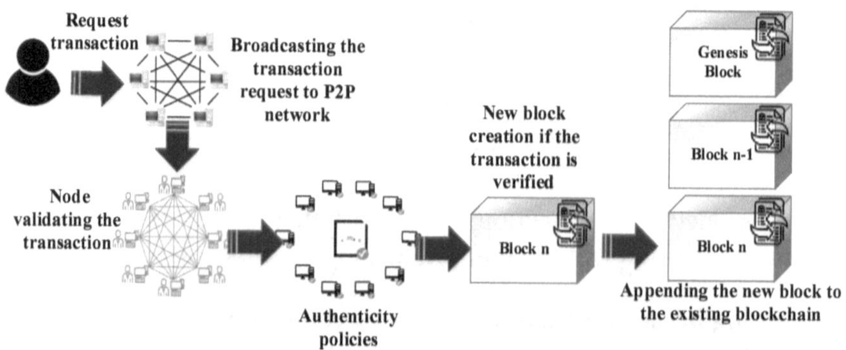

Figure 2.7: Blockchain Mining Process

In order to verify the authenticity of the encrypted data, it is necessary to decode it. The process of decrypting the data that is encoded in blocks is a difficult task that requires the utilization of computational hardware and software, in addition to the utilization of human effort. There is a possibility that decoding a single piece of data will need a large amount of time and effort from both the computer and the person who is involved. The successful decryption of the data is dependent on a combination of computing speed and human intelligence, which, when combined with adjacent blocks, verifies the transaction. As a result, the data can be successfully processed as shown in figure 2.7. The bitcoin blocks link together by codes named hash-codes. These hash codes meet specific requirements in the encrypted data's solution.

Miners must solve complex problems to find the optimal solution hash that corresponds with the given data. The resolution to the hidden code encryption is known as the "Proof of Work." This term reflects the significant resources, time, and energy invested by the miner. Generating this proof of work is challenging and can sometimes result in lower profitability. The sequential process of blockchain mining is as follows:

a) Token dispatch:

When a user wants to conduct a transaction that involves only a few fees inside the community, parties/node/user sends tokens to other parties/node/users from the utility wallets in their devices (process of distributing tokens to users or participants within a blockchain network). The methodologies and procedures related to token distribution are crucial for ensuring a successful and compliant blockchain environment.

b) Broadcasting of Transaction:

In order for a blockchain network to function properly, broadcasting transactions is an essential stage within the process. Blockchain dissemination refers to a procedure that requires the dissemination of transaction information to all nodes within the network, enabling those nodes to confirm, record, and preserve the integrity of the blockchain. To ensure that blockchain networks continue to maintain their decentralized nature, broadcasting transactions is absolutely necessary. It ensures that all nodes receive notifications of new transactions, simplifying the validation and inclusion of these transactions in the blockchain. When it comes to the overall performance and security of blockchain systems, the efficiency and dependability of transaction broadcasting are two of the most important factors.

c)   Selection of a transaction for a block:

A blockchain network must have a mechanism that chooses which transactions to include in a block. This process has a direct impact on the efficiency and efficacy of the blockchain. Once the transactions broadcast and remain in the mempool for confirmation, the selection process commences. When it comes to blockchain technology, the process of selecting transactions for a block is extremely important since it has an effect on the speed of transactions, the efficiency of the network, and the profitability of miners. Miners have the ability to improve their decisions by taking into consideration factors such as transaction fees, size, and the consensus mechanism of the blockchain. This helps to ensure that the network is both balanced and efficient throughout its operation. This approach guarantees timely confirmation of transactions and rewards miners for their efforts.

d)   Mining the signature and Formation of block:

Miners select transactions and group them together to form a new block. Before adding the block to the blockchain, a signature is now required. This signature is referred to as "Proof of Work." A signature or proof of work (PoW) represents that a miner has spent a certain amount of time and resources solving extremely difficult mathematical problems. Each block of transactions has unique mathematical problems to solve; each miner will work on a problem that is unique to the block they built. Every mathematical problem is complex and necessitates a large amount of computational work, resulting in a wide range of energy inputs. Mining is the activity of resolving a complex problem through mathematical calculation. Mining is the process of obtaining a block's signature.

e)   Addition of block in to the blockchain:

The miner will inform the other miners about this block and its signature if they receive the certified output or signature for the next block before anyone else.

f)   Verification of signatures legitimacy:

To verify the miner's signature, other miners will hash the broadcast block's string and compare it to the signature. If it suits, the miners offer their confirmation of its validity. A higher number of confirmations makes it more difficult for hackers to operate on the system. This clarifies the definition of "proof of work." The signature is the 'evidence' of the work executed in the form of the computational calculations. The network now prepares the block for inclusion in the blockchain and distributes it among all the nodes. The various nodes will receive and store the information.

g)   Confirmation depends:

The term "confirmation" refers to each block that follows the most recent block in the blockchain. For instance, if function 06 adds a new block to the blockchain, and the total length of the blockchain is 9, then the confirmation blocks for the 06 block are (607 to 609) = 3. Each time a new block enters the blockchain, the miners must begin at step 3 by assembling a new block of transactions.

Test your skills

1.   What is block? Define the structure of block in blockchain.

2.   What is the genesis block?

3.   Discuss the various component of block in blockchain. Write the utility of every component.

4.   Explain the Blockchain Mining Process in detail.

5.   What is transaction? Discuss the Transaction Validation Process.

6.   Discuss the various Scripting or programming language used in Blockchain Technology.

7.   What is block mining? Discuss the various types of block mining.

8.   What is virtual machine in blockchain?

Chapter – 3

WORKING MECHANISM OF BLOCKCHAIN

The objective of this chapter is to examine the relationship between distributed computing and blockchain technology, as well as to conduct a thorough analysis of the architecture and utilization of blockchain technology. This chapter provides an explanation of the key elements of a blockchain network and their function. The overview of the various phases of blockchain functionality is also provided. It is also illustrated that publishing of a distributed log of the committed transactions using a consensus process to perform secure communication between untrusted nodes. The network's step-by-step operation is then described in general.

"In the context of blockchain technology, decentralization pertains to the process of shifting authority and decision-making power from a centralized entity, such as an individual, organization, or group, to a network that is distributed across multiple participants".

The concept of decentralization is not a recent development. When developing a technological solution, it is customary to evaluate three main network architectures: centralized, distributed, and decentralized.

3.1 Decentralization

Decentralization refers to the distribution of functions, power, and information rather than their centralization in a single location. The primary purpose of decentralizing in blockchains is to prevent concentration of control in the hands of a select few. Instead, several nodes maintain the network, making it decentralized. Decentralized blockchains design data to be unchangeable and irreversible once entered. You cannot edit or alter old data, but you can add new data. This is one of the most crucial aspects of blockchain technology, ensuring its flawless functioning. You can store anything, from cryptocurrencies to important data, contracts, or other valuable digital assets. With the aid of blockchain technology, you can exercise direct control over these assets using your private key. Therefore, the decentralized structure is restoring power and rights to the common people over their assets. Figure 3.2 provides a simple example. How this blockchain feature is truly making changes.

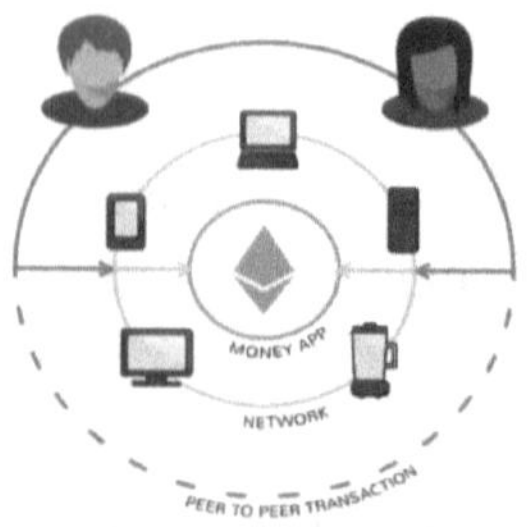

Figure 3.1 Decentralization Application

3.1.1 characteristics of decentralized system

a) **Minimum Failure:** The blockchain is meticulously organized, and due to its independence from human calculations, it exhibits a high level of fault tolerance. Therefore, this system does not typically experience accidental failures.

b) **User Control:** The decentralized system gives users the ability to take command. Individually, they are able to manage their assets without relying on any third party. Each one of them is capable of carrying out the task on their own while simultaneously performing it.

c) **Minimum Prone to Breakdown:** Decentralization, a fundamental characteristic of blockchain technology, enables it to withstand malicious assaults. The difficulty and cost associated with hacking the system are significant. Consequently, it is less prone to malfunction.

d) **No Third-Party:** Because of the decentralized structure of the technology, it is able to function without requiring the assistance of a third party, so removing the additional risks that are associated with intermediaries.

e) **Zero Scams:** Due of the system's reliance on algorithms, individuals cannot mislead. The blockchain is not accessible for individual business.

f) **Transparency:** The technology's decentralized characteristic promotes a transparent and accessible profile for every member. Every modification on the blockchain is transparent, so augmenting its robustness.

g) **Authentic Nature:** The system's features make it unique for people of every kind. Hackers will encounter significant difficulties in their attempts to breach security.

3.1.2 Benefits of Decentralization

a) *Provides a trustless environment*

In a decentralized blockchain network, no one must know or trust anyone else. Each member of the network has a copy of the exact same data in the form of a distributed ledger. Most of the other members in the network will reject a member's altered or corrupted ledger. Blockchain creates a trustless environment by eliminating the need for intermediaries. Cryptographic proof and consensus mechanisms establish trust, allowing participants to interact directly without relying on a central authority or third party to verify or guarantee transactions.

b) *Improves data reconciliation*

Blockchain enhances data reconciliation by providing a single, transparent, and immutable ledger that all participants can access. The network records and updates all transactions in real-time, minimizing discrepancies between different parties and ensuring everyone has consistent and synchronized data, eliminating the need for manual reconciliation processes. Each party typically transforms and stores this data, only for it to resurface during downstream transmission. Transforming data increases the likelihood of data loss or incorrect data entering the work stream. With a decentralized data repository, each entity has access to a shared, real-time view of the data.

c) *Reduces points of weakness*

Decentralization can mitigate vulnerabilities in systems that overly depend on certain entities. These vulnerabilities may result in systemic problems, including the failure to provide promised services or the delivery of inferior services due to resource exhaustion, bottlenecks, inadequate incentives for quality, or corruption.

d) *Optimizes resource distribution*

Decentralization can facilitate the equitable allocation of resources, resulting in enhanced and more dependable service delivery while reducing the likelihood of disaster.

3.1.3 Issues with Decentralization

Decentralization can have several issues, including:

a) Coordination and Decision-Making:

In decentralized systems, decision-making frequently necessitates consensus among several players. This can impede procedures and make it difficult to respond swiftly to changes or issues. Obtaining consensus can be difficult, especially in large-scale networks with various players. Without a central authority to adjudicate conflicts, disagreements among participants can cause the network to fracture. For example, in blockchain systems, this can cause forks, in which the network separates into different versions, possibly confusing users and separating resources.

b) Scalability Issues:

High latency and limited throughput are the most significant challenges associated with decentralization. Many decentralized systems, particularly those employing consensus algorithms such as Proof of Work (PoW) or Proof of Stake (PoS), face challenges in achieving efficient scalability. In contrast to centralized systems, they are capable of processing only a restricted number of transactions or operations each second. This limits their capacity to manage widespread, international acceptance. Decentralized systems frequently experience increased latency because they require consensus among a distributed network. Transaction times increase due to the prolonged process of verifying and propagating data across all nodes.

c) Security Risks:

51% Attacks in decentralized systems can occur when a single organization or group controls more than half of the network's resources, such as the processing power in blockchain, giving them the ability to manipulate the system. This could result in double spending or changes to transaction history, putting the system's integrity at risk. The coding of smart contracts introduces additional security risks. Decentralized systems that use smart contracts, like Ethereum, may be vulnerable to code faults or exploitation. These difficulties are difficult to address once the contract has been deployed, as modifications may require consensus or be irreversible.

d) Accountability:

It is difficult to develop trust or hold individuals accountable for their activities in many decentralized systems because participants are allowed to remain pseudonymous; this makes it difficult to establish trust. When bad actors take advantage of this anonymity, they are able to commit fraudulent acts or malevolent activities without fear of repercussions. The central authority that was responsible for monitoring, regulation, and responsibility is eliminated through the process of decentralization. When something goes wrong, such as when there is fraud, when there is a hack, or when there is a failure in the system, this can be an issue.

3.1.4 Limitations of Decentralized Blockchain

Decentralized blockchains present various benefits, including security, transparency, and the removal of intermediaries; however, they also have specific limitations:

a) Scalability

Scalability is one of the most serious challenges for blockchain networks. Due to scalability, we can increase the number of nodes or participants in the blockchain network with minimum effort. However, as transaction volumes and demand for decentralized apps increase, blockchain networks struggle to process transactions efficiently, leading to bottlenecks, higher fees, and slower confirmation times.

b) Self-Maintenance

The process of maintaining a blockchain network is a continuous and resource-intensive endeavour. In contrast to traditional systems, blockchains are decentralized, relying on a network of participants rather than a single authority to manage and maintain their functions. Consistent upgrades and supervision are crucial for safeguarding the network's integrity and functionality. These responsibilities encompass transaction verification, block addition, and overall system security. Participants, especially miners in Proof of Work (PoW) systems, necessitate considerable processing power and energy for this maintenance.

c) Storage

As blockchain networks increase and manage a higher volume of transactions, their storage demands escalate significantly. Each node in the network must maintain a complete copy of the blockchain, resulting in significant data requirements. Extensive blockchains with substantial transaction histories often face significant challenges, resulting in increased operational expenses due to the need for enhanced storage capacity and robust infrastructure. The storage requirements may dissuade individual users or smaller enterprises from engaging in the network, potentially restricting the quantity of full nodes.

d) Interoperability

Interoperability in blockchain denotes the ability of various blockchain networks to communicate and interact effectively. However, accomplishing this is challenging as each blockchain functions on its unique protocols and standards. This challenge significantly restricts the technology's potential for broader applications, including global trade and cross-platform collaborations. Unlocking the full potential of blockchain requires the development of standards and protocols that enable seamless interaction among different blockchain networks.

3.2 Distributed System

The most dramatic change in information technology over the past two decades has been the expansion of networked workstations and the decline of the central mainframe. This change has distributed hardware resources and given end users access to more processing power. Connecting computers to a network allows the network to harness the combined power of all connected computers to tackle challenging tasks. Networks of processing nodes can perform computations in two categories: centralized or distributed. We must designate one node to locally process the entire application in a central system, which all users constantly share. As a result, there is only 1 point of failure and 1 point of control. The availability of inexpensive, high-performance computers and network tools is driving the growth of decentralized computing. When a few powerful computers connect and communicate with each other, they can unleash an astoundingly large total computing power. The performance share of such a system may be higher than that of a single supercomputer. Computerized sharing, A decentralized computing strategy has the potential to be very effective for accessing significant amounts of computational power. Cost-effective communication and computation are the main goals of such systems. Cost-effective communication and computation are the main goals of such systems. Distributed systems divide the application's processing steps among the participating nodes. The idea of communication between computers is the fundamental step in all distributed computing architectures. A distributed system is a program that implements a set of protocols to synchronize the activities of numerous processes on a communication network so that all parts work together to complete a single or a limited number of related tasks. Through the communication network, the cooperating computers can access both local and remote resources in the distributed system. In a distributed system, the user is unaware that there are numerous autonomous computers. Numerous computers, located in various distant locations, carry out the jobs without the user's knowledge. This suggests that, akin to systems under central control, no single computer within the system bears the full burden of the resources required to execute a computer program.

 *A typical distributed system will consist of a significant number of interconnected devices that each run their own programmes but are influenced by messages, shared memory updates, or the states of other devices. Distributed systems are distinguished by their structure. A single client communicating with a single server is a simple example of a distributed system, while large, amorphous networks like the Internet as a whole are examples of distributed systems.*

3.2.1 Distributed System Architecture

Understanding distributed systems is essential to understanding blockchain because, at its core, blockchain is a distributed system. More precisely, it is a decentralized, distributed system. A distributed system is a computing paradigm in which two or more nodes cooperate with everyone to achieve a common goal. We create the model to make the system appear to end users as a single logical platform. In the real world, almost every distributed system relies on interactions between clients and servers. Here, one process, known as the client, sends a request to another, known as the server. The server then sends a response back to the client. We can use our asynchronous message passing model to represent this interaction by describing how the client and the server handle transitions.

The term "node" refers to a single member in a distributed system. Each node can communicate with other nodes by sending and receiving messages from them. Nodes can be reliable, mistaken, or malignant; they have their own memory and processor. Byzantine refers to a node that can behave as it pleases. This random behavior could be the result of malevolent intent, which is harmful for the network's performance. We generally refer to any unexpected behavior of a network node as byzantine behavior.

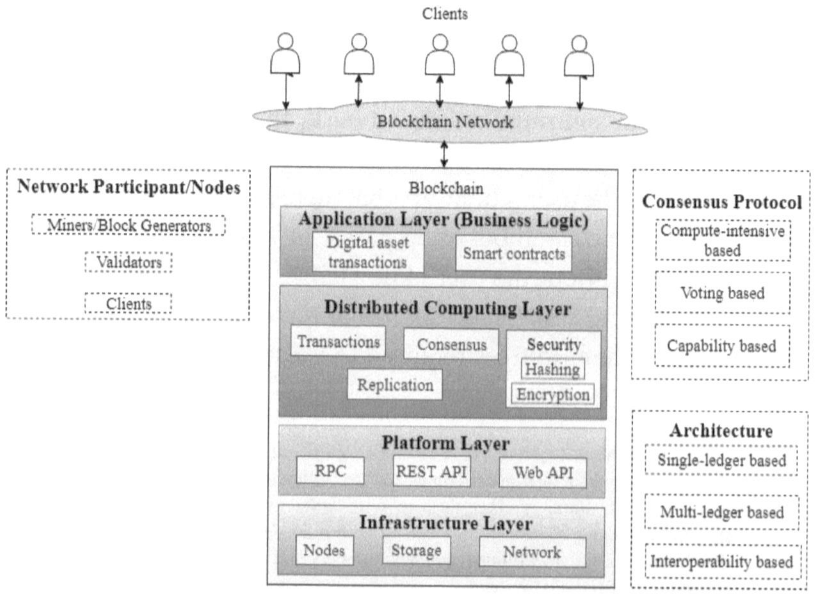

Fig: 3.2 Distributed architecture of Blockchain Application

Figure 3.2 divides the blockchain architecture into four layers: infrastructure, platform, distributed computing, and application. The infrastructure layer includes all the necessary hardware components for running the blockchain, including nodes, storage, and network facilities. The nodes are network participants. In a typical blockchain network, there are three distinct types of nodes: simple nodes (also known as light nodes), full nodes, and mining nodes. A basic node in the network is only responsible for sending and receiving transactions. It does not store a copy of the ledger or validate transactions. On the other hand, a full node is capable of both storing a copy of the ledger and validating transactions. A mining node, also known as a block generator, is a type of full node that has the ability to mine. Mining refers to the process of generating a new block. The storage component is responsible for storing the ledger of transaction records. The platform layer enables the use of Remote Procedure Calls (RPC).

3.2.2 Characteristics of a Distributed System

A distributed system is a group of independent computers that collaborate to accomplish a shared objective. Here are some key characteristics of distributed systems:

a)   Fault-Tolerant:

Various hardware and software components make up distributed systems. These component failures can lead to service disruptions. Therefore, the system must be able to recover from failures without executing incorrect operations or causing further issues. The objective of fault tolerance is to prevent system breakdowns even when faults exist, resulting in uninterrupted service. Fault tolerance is defined as a system's ability to disguise the presence of fault. The reliability of a system is defined as the probability that it survives until that time. A reliable system prevents loss of information even in the event of component failures. Fault tolerance is typically achieved through redundancy, which refers to components of a system that are not required for normal operation but serve as backups. We can classify redundancy into three types: hardware, software, and time.

i)   **Hardware redundancy** involves adding extra physical components to the system. These additional components take over when a failure occurs in the primary ones.

ii) **Software redundancy** includes supplementary code and instructions that manage the extra hardware, ensuring it operates smoothly during a failure to maintain uninterrupted service.

iii) **Time redundancy** involves executing the same instruction multiple times to ensure correctness in case of transient errors.

The goal of fault tolerance is to avoid failures in the system even in the presence of faults. The aim of any fault tolerant system is to increase its reliability or availability. Redundancy is achieved by adding extra hardware components which take over the role of failed components in case some faults occur.

Blockchain applications use Byzantine fault tolerance, a complex type of fault tolerance, to maintain system continuity and functionality in the event of a fault or failure. It refers to the capacity of a network or system to continue functioning despite the failure or malfunction of certain components. With a BFT system, blockchain networks continue to function or execute predetermined actions so long as most network participants are trustworthy and authentic. Byzantine fault tolerance in blockchain technology derives from Leslie Lamport, Marshall Pease, and Robert Shostak's work on the Byzantine general problem.

b) Scalable:

Even when some aspects of a distributed system scale to larger sizes, it can still function correctly. Scale refers to the number of users, entities, distant nodes, and organizations that manage various parts of the system. The three elements of scale affect distributed systems in many ways. Among the components affected are naming, authentication, authorization, communication, the use of remote resources, and the mechanisms by which users observe the system. We employ three techniques to manage scale: replication, distribution, and caching. Replication creates multiple copies of resources. Its use in naming, authentication, and file services reduces the load on individual servers and improves the reliability and availability of the services as a whole. Placing the replicas and maintaining their consistency are two crucial aspects of replication. The placement of replicas in a distributed system depends on the purpose of reproducing the resource. The system scatters the replicas when replicating a service to minimize network delays during access. If the majority of users are local and the service is being replicated to improve its availability or spread the load across multiple servers, then replicas may be placed near one another. Everyone in the system should notice any changes made to the object. For example, the system sends the updates to any replica, and that replica forwards them to the others as they become available. When different replicas receive inconsistent updates in different orders, they use timestamps (the date/time of update generation) to distinguish between the copies. Distribution, another mechanism for managing scale in distributed systems, enables a distributed service to extend its information across several servers. By distributing data across multiple servers, each server can maintain a smaller database, thereby reducing the time required for database searches. Distribution also distributes the load among the servers, thereby minimizing the number of requests each handles. Distributing requests to servers based on their power allows for effective management of the server load. Assigning data to servers near their most frequently used locations can reduce network traffic. If subordinate servers have cached copies, we can avoid the upper levels in a tree-structured system. Caching is another important technique for building scalable systems. Caching decreases the load on servers and the network. You can access cached data faster than when you make a new request. The difference between replication and caching is that cached data is short-term. Instead of propagating updates on cached data, consistency is maintained by nullifying cached data when consistency cannot be guaranteed. The client typically performs caching, which reduces the frequency of requests to network services. Caching can also occur on the servers executing those services. Reading a file from the cached copy in memory on the file server is faster than reading it from the client's local disk.

Scale refers to the number of users, entities, distant nodes, and organizations managing various parts of the system. Three techniques to manage scale include replication, distribution, and caching. Replication creates multiple copies of resources, reducing the load on individual servers and improving service reliability. Placement and consistency are crucial aspects of replication. Distribution allows a distributed service to extend its information across multiple servers, reducing database searches and managing server load. Caching decreases the load on servers and the network, allowing faster access to cached data. Caching maintains consistency by nullifying cached data when consistency cannot be guaranteed. Both replication and caching can occur on the servers executing services, reducing the frequency of requests and improving performance.

c) Predictable Performance:

Performance is determined through several kinds of metrics, such as response time (the interval from the completion of a request to the start of a response), throughput (the speed at which data is sent or received over a network), system utilization, and network capacity. Consistently responding with the expected speed and efficiency demonstrates reliable performance.

d) Openness:

The characteristic of 'openness' guarantees that a subsystem remains consistently open to interactions with other systems. Web services are software systems created to facilitate smooth machine-to-machine communication across a network. These protocols facilitate the expansion and enhancement of distributed systems. An open system that scales offers advantages compared to a fully closed and self-sufficient system. A distributed system that is independent of the heterogeneity present in the underlying environment, including hardware and software platforms, attains the characteristic of openness. Consequently, all services are uniformly available to every client, whether local or remote, within the system. The implementation, installation, and debugging of new services should be relatively straightforward in a system with openness characteristics.

e) Security:

Distributed systems should allow communication between programs, users, and resources on different computers by enforcing necessary security arrangements. The main purpose of the security features is to ensure confidentiality, integrity, and availability. Confidentiality (privacy) is protection against disclosure to an unauthorized person. The violations of confidentiality range from uncomfortable to catastrophic. Integrity provides protection against alteration and corruption. Availability keeps the resource accessible. Many incidents of hacking compromise the integrity of databases and other resources. Attacks against availability are known as "denial of service" attacks. Other important security concerns are access control and nonrepudiation. Ensuring access control allows users to access only the resources and services to which they have the right. Additionally, it guarantees the users' legitimate access to resources. Nonrepudiation provides protection against denial by one of the entities involved in a communication. The security mechanisms put into practice should guarantee appropriate use of resources by different users in the system.

f) Transparency:

Users and application developers should perceive distributed systems as a whole, not as a collection of cooperating components. Users remain unaware of the locations of the computer systems involved in operations, concurrent operations, data replication, resource discovery from multiple sites, failures, system recovery, etc. Transparency hides the distributed nature of the system from its users and shows them that it is appearing and performing as a normal centralized system. A distributed system can employ transparency in various ways:

i) Access transparency enables users of a distributed system to access local and remote resources using identical operations. (e.g., navigation in the web).

ii) Location transparency describes names used to identify network resources (e.g., an IP address) independent of both the user's location and the resource location. In other words, location transparency allows a user to access resources from anywhere on the network without knowing where they are located. A file could be on the user's own PC or thousands of miles away on other servers.

iii) Concurrency transparency enables several processes to operate concurrently using shared information objects without interference between them (e.g., an automatic teller machine network). Users won't notice other users in the system (even if they share resources).

iv) Replication transparency enables the system to make additional copies of files and other resources for the purpose of performance and/or reliability without the users noticing. Replicating a resource across multiple locations should present it to the user as a single resource, with mirror sites serving as reliable sources for large downloads.

v) Failure transparency enables the applications to complete their task despite failures occurring in certain components of the system. For instance, when a server malfunctions but automatically redirects users to another server, the system demonstrates high failure transparency.

Failure transparency is one of the most difficult types to accomplish since it is hard to determine whether a server has actually failed or whether it is simply responding very slowly. Moreover, it is generally unfeasible to achieve full failure transparency in a distributed system since networks are unreliable.

vi) Migration transparency enables the transfer of resources from one location to another without the need for name changes. (e.g., Web pages). Users should not be aware of whether a resource or computing entity possesses the ability to move to a different physical or logical location.

vii) Performance transparency ensures the load variation should not lead to performance degradation. Automatic reconfiguration in response to load changes could achieve this. (e.g., load distribution)

3.3.3 Benefits of Distributed Systems

Distributed systems provide several benefits compared to monolithic or single systems, such as:

a) **Flexibility:**Enhancing processing power becomes more feasible as the demand for services increases. Today, we can dynamically integrate servers into a distributed system in many instances.

b) **Scalability**: Distributed systems can scale horizontally with ease by incorporating additional nodes to manage increased workloads or traffic.

c) **Fault Tolerance and Reliability**: Distributing tasks across multiple nodes enhances the resilience of distributed systems to failures. When a single node experiences failure, the remaining nodes are able to maintain functionality, thereby enhancing the overall reliability of the system.

d) **Resource Sharing**: Nodes in a distributed system can share resources such as storage, computing power, and data, allowing for more efficient utilization and collaboration.

e) **Improved Performance**: Workload distribution across multiple nodes can enhance performance by parallelizing tasks and reducing processing time.

f) **Geographical Distribution**: Distributed systems can operate across various geographic locations, allowing for global collaboration and providing localized services closer to users, reducing latency.

g) **Modularity: Distributed systems typically allow for component updates, replacements, or expansions without affecting the system as a whole.**

h) **Availability**: With redundancy and replication, distributed systems can provide higher availability, ensuring that services remain operational even during outages or failures in parts of the system.

3.3.4 Challenges of Distributed Systems

Distributed systems are significantly more complex than monolithic computer environments, and they present a number of design, operational, and maintenance issues. This includes:

a) Increased Opportunities for Failure: The number of systems added to a computing environment increases the likelihood of failure. A single node crash in a poorly designed system can bring down the entire system. Despite the fault-tolerant design of distributed systems, it is neither automatic nor foolproof.

b) Challenges in the synchronization process: In order to ensure that processes are properly synchronized, distributed systems that lack a global clock require meticulous programming to prevent transmission delays that can result in data corruption and errors. Synchronization can be difficult in a complex system, such as a multiplayer video game, and is particularly difficult on a public network that transports data traffic.

c) Network Issues: Distributed systems rely on networks for communication, making them vulnerable to network delays, congestion, and partitioning, which can affect system performance and reliability.

d) Consistency: Maintaining data consistency across distributed nodes, especially in real-time applications, is challenging. Techniques like replication can complicate ensuring that all nodes have the same data at the same time.

e) Fault Handling: While distributed systems are fault-tolerant, detecting and managing faults, especially in complex systems, can be difficult. Ensuring smooth recovery from node or network failures requires sophisticated mechanisms.

3.4 Decentralized Mechanism of Blockchain Application

As mentioned earlier, one of the primary characteristics of any blockchain application is that it can operate in a decentralized or distributed manner. Blockchain works via a multistep process. All of these steps are carried out in the order depicted in Figure 3.3.

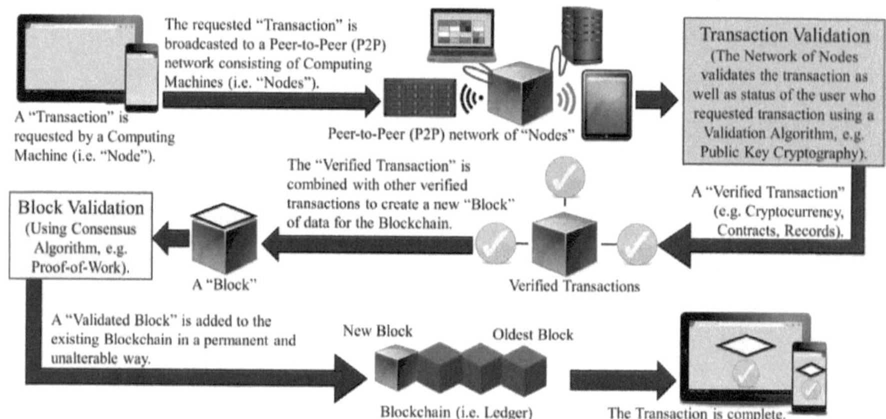

Figure 3.3: Working mode of blockchain

Step1: Facilitating a transaction: A new transaction is added to the blockchain network (peer-to-peer networks) Using public and private keys, all the data that needs to be communicated is double encrypted.

Step 2: Verification of transaction: The transaction is subsequently transmitted to a network of peer-to-peer computers that are distributed worldwide for verification. Every node on the network will verify the transaction's validity.

Step 3: Formation of a new block: In a typical blockchain network, there are multiple nodes that work together to verify numerous transactions simultaneously, leading to the formation of a new block. After the verification process confirms the legitimacy of the transaction, it will be included in the mempool. At a specific node, all the verified transactions are collected in a mempool. Multiple mempools then come together to form a block. i.e This action generates a block that represents a particular transaction or data.

Step 4: Consensus Algorithm: The consensus algorithm makes sure that all nodes work together to add a new block to the blockchain, which makes it an ever-present part of the network. However, permitting each node to add blocks independently would disrupt the blockchain's functionality. Nodes use a consensus mechanism to prevent this, ensuring that each newly added block represents a single, universally accepted version of the truth, agreed upon by all nodes. This mechanism also guarantees the secure appending of only valid blocks to the blockchain. Miners, the nodes selected to add a block, receive rewards for their efforts. The consensus algorithm also generates a unique hash code for each block, which is essential for adding it to the blockchain.

Step 5: Block addition to blockchain: Once the newly created block has obtained its hash value and has been authenticated, it is now prepared to be added to the blockchain. Each block in a blockchain contains a hash value of the previous block, which serves as a cryptographic link between the blocks. A new block is added to the open end of the blockchain.

Steps 6: Transaction complete: The transaction has been successfully completed. Once the block is added to the blockchain, the transaction details are permanently secured. This means that the updated blockchain, containing the new transaction, is distributed across the network, effectively finalising the transaction.

3.4.1 Ledger

A ledger maintains records of transactions. In the past, people used pen and paper to maintain ledgers, which allowed them to monitor the exchange of products and services. Currently, a centralized trusted third party, known as the ledger proprietor, digitally manages extensive databases on behalf of a community of users. One server or a coordinated cluster of servers can implement these centralized ledgers in a distributed manner.

3.4.2 Problems with Exiting Business Ledgers

The current business-related ledgers have several deficiencies. These systems exhibit inefficiency, high costs, and vulnerability to misuse and tampering. Disputes arise due to a lack of transparency, which renders the system vulnerable to corruption and fraud. The process of resolving disputes, potentially reversing transactions, and offering insurance for transactions incurs significant costs. The presence of these risks and uncertainties has a detrimental impact on the ability to capitalize on business possibilities.

In addition, out-of-sync versions of business ledgers on each network participant's individual system result in erroneous business decisions based on temporary, inaccurate data. At best, the reconciliation of different copies of the ledgers delays the ability to make a fully informed decision.

There is a growing interest in exploring distributed ownership of the ledger. Blockchain technology enables such an approach using both distributed ownership as well as a distributed physical architecture. The distributed physical architecture of blockchain networks often involves a much larger set of computers than is typical for centrally managed distributed physical architecture. The growing interest in distributed ownership of ledgers is due to possible trust, security, and reliability concerns related to ledgers with centralized ownership. Users must trust that the owner is adequately backing up the system to prevent the loss or destruction of centrally owned ledgers.

3.4.3 Distributed Ledger

A blockchain network is inherently distributed, generating several backup copies that concurrently update and synchronize the identical ledger data among participants / peers (figure 3.4 shows the concept of decentralized ledgers). A principal advantage of blockchain technology is that each user can retain an individual copy of the ledger. When new full nodes join the blockchain network, they seek to identify other full nodes and request a complete copy of the blockchain ledger, further complicating the loss or destruction of the ledger. Some blockchain implementations include the functionality to facilitate private transactions or private channels. Private transactions enable the dissemination of information exclusively to the nodes involved in a transaction, rather than to the entire network.

Distributed Ledgers

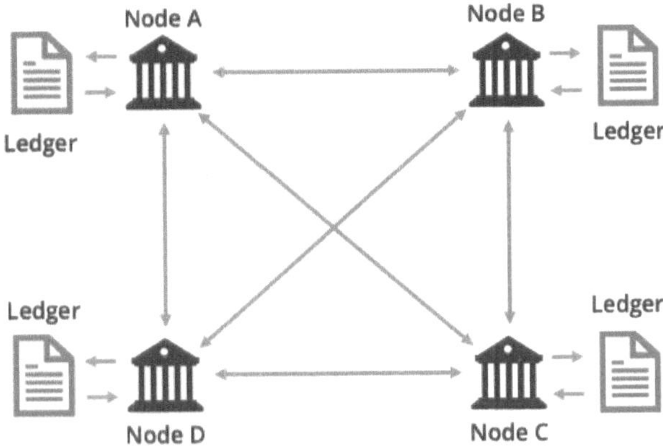

Figure 3.4: Distributed Ledgers

A distributed ledger refers to a specific type of database that is shared, replicated, and synchronised among the participants of a decentralised network. The distributed ledger is responsible for recording transactions among the participants in the network, including the exchange of assets or data.

3.4.4 Shared Ledger

Shared ledgers are similar to distributed records. The public or an organization can share this application or database. A shared, permissioned ledger is the append-only system of records (SOR) and a single source of truth. It is visible to the authenticated members in the business network channels. Multiple parties distribute a shared ledger, a type of database, enabling them to access and update a common record of transactions. A distributed ledger blockchain disperses the ledger among all its participants, enabling it to span multiple organizations. Instead of sorting blocks, a distributed ledger stores records concurrently, allowing them to be both private and public. Usually, a public ledger will provide every piece of information about a transaction and the participant. It's all out in the open; there is nowhere to hide. The situation with private or linked blockchains differs slightly. However, in these scenarios, a large number of individuals have access to the real-time information in the ledger. This is because all network users maintain the ledger. The system distributes computational power among the computers to achieve optimal results. This is why it's considered a crucial aspect of blockchain technology. The result will always be a more efficient ledger system that can take on the traditional ones.

> *Shared ledgers are applications or databases that allow multiple parties to share and update transactions. They are similar to distributed records and are visible to authenticated members in business networks.*

3.4.5 Centralized Vs Distributed Ledger

Figure 3.5 illustrates the differences between centralized and distributed ledgers. The following are the key distinctions between centralized and distributed ledgers:

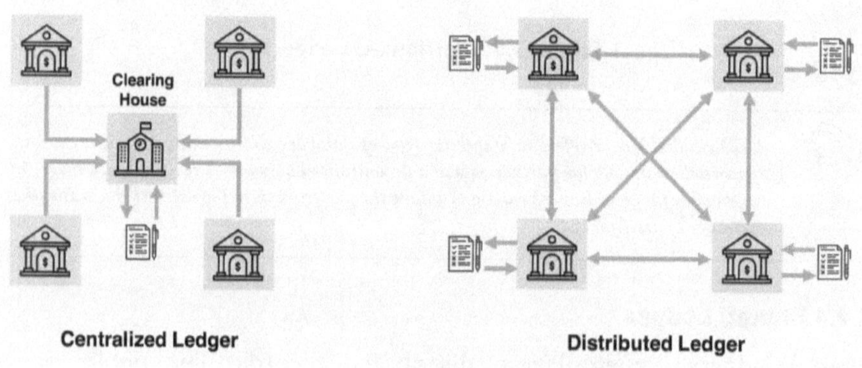

Fig 3.5: Centralized Ledger Distributed Ledgers

Centralized Ledger	Distributed Ledger
A homogeneous network may host a centralized ledger, in which all software, hardware, and network infrastructure are identical. This feature has the potential to reduce the overall system's resilience, as an attack on a single network segment would have a significant influence on the entire system.	*A distributed ledger may be on a heterogeneous network, where the software and network infrastructure are all different. An attack on one node on the blockchain network may not guarantee success on other nodes due to the many differences between them.*
A user must trust that the owner is validating each received transaction because the transactions on a centralized ledger are not transparent.	*In Distributed Ledger, check that all transactions are valid; if a malicious node were transmitting invalid transactions, others would detect and ignore them, preventing the invalid transactions from propagating throughout the blockchain network.*

Centralized Ledger	Distributed Ledger
In Centralized Ledger, transaction list may not be complete; a user must trust that the owner is including all valid transactions that have been received.	*In Distributed Ledger all accepted transactions create a new block, a reference must be made to a previous block – therefore building on top of it. If a publishing node did not include a reference to the latest block, other nodes would reject it.*
In Centralized Ledger, transaction data may have been altered. Possibility of tempering is high.	*In Distributed Ledger use cryptographic mechanisms such as digital signatures and cryptographic hash functions to provide tamper evident and tamper resistant ledgers.*
A centralized ledger system may be insecure; a user must trust the associated computer systems and networks. The implementation of critical security patches adheres to best practices for enhanced security. A breach in the system could lead to the theft of personal information.	*Due to the distributed nature of ledgers, there is no centralized point of attack. Generally, information on a blockchain network is publicly viewable and offers nothing to steal.*

3.4.6 Why Ledger is Important Features of Blockchain?

One of the fundamental features of blockchain technology is the ledger. Here are some reasons why the ledger is important to blockchain and how it works with the rest of the system:

a) No Malicious Changes: The distributed ledger effectively addresses any anomalous activity or tampering.

b) Responsibility for Verification: In this case, nodes in the system act as verifiers. Other users would need to verify the transaction before adding it.

c) No Extra Favors: No one on the network can get any special favors from the network.

3.5 Distributed Ledger Technology

Distributed ledger technology has the potential to significantly enhance record keeping by altering the core principles of how organizations gather and exchange data for their ledgers. Distributed ledger technology (DLT) refers to the technological infrastructure and protocols that enable simultaneous access, validation, and record updating across a networked database. DLT, or distributed ledger technology, serves as the foundation for blockchains. This infrastructure enables users to easily track and identify any modifications made to the data, thereby minimizing the necessity for data audits. Moreover, DLT ensures the reliability of the data and restricts access only to authorized individuals who require it.

DLTs enable the secure and exact storage of data using cryptography. We can gain access to the data using "keys" and cryptographic signatures. Once information is stored, it can become an immutable database; the ledger is governed by the network's rules, which are coded into the database programming.

a) Distribution Ledger Technology (DLT) is a new and growing way to store and exchange data across several data stores. Each ledger includes identical data entries stored and controlled by a distributed network of computer servers called nodes. Describe DLT as a distributed database with special features.

b) DLT stores asset transactions and information in multiple locations concurrently. Unlike databases, distributed ledgers have no central data repository or administrative services.

c) Each distributed ledger node studies and validates each item, documenting and agreeing its legitimacy. A distributed ledger may hold static and dynamic data like financial transactions.

3.5.1 Distributed Ledger Vs Distributed Ledger Technology

Distributed Ledger Technology (DLT) is centered on a distributed and encoded database where transaction records are maintained. A distributed ledger is a database that is distributed across multiple computers, nodes, institutions, or countries and is accessible to multiple individuals worldwide.

3.5.2 Benefits of Distributed Ledger Technology (DLT)

a) Distributed Ledger Technology (DLT) offers several advantages over traditional ledger systems. Because DLT is a decentralized system, there is no centralized point of failure or control. This makes DLT more attack-resistant and less susceptible to system-wide failures.

b) DLT simplifies the process of viewing data and transactions, enabling all users to understand how the system operates.

c)   DLT eliminates intermediaries and automates transactions with smart contracts. Smart contracts can automatically execute when criteria are satisfied, reducing human contact and administration. This cuts expenses and boosts efficiency.

3.5.3 Drawback of Distributed Ledger Technology

i)   DLT has many drawbacks. DLT is still complicated to deploy and maintain.

ii)   As the number of participants and transactions on a DLT network grows, scalability may become problematic. As a result, DLT processes may result in delayed processing capabilities or higher costs associated with their utilization.

iii)   Finally, DLT's immutability can be a strength and a drawback. Since all transactions are public, sensitive transactions may be difficult to hide. Errors or fraud can make transactions harder to correct or reverse.

Pros	Cons
Spreads systematic risk around, minimizing the risk of a single point of failure	*Is more complex compared to more traditional ledger solutions*
Has greater security due to cryptographic algorithms	*Often requires higher energy consumption for operation*
Allows for transparency and visibility into operations	*May have difficult scaling as more users/ transactions occur*
May prove to be more efficient due to smart contract automation	*Still remains risky due to lack of regulation*
Offers individuals with limited access to traditional systems potentially greater capabilities	*May prove to be difficult to reverse fraudulent or erroneous activity*

Test your skill

1.   Write the difference between decentralization and distributed networks.

2.   Explain the concept of Decentralization. How can we implement the Decentralized network?

3.   Write the Characteristics of a Distributed System.

4.   What are the challenges associated with Distributed System?

5.   What is ledger? Discuss the Problems with current business ledgers.

6. Write the benefits of Distributed ledger.

7. Explain the Distributed architecture of Blockchain Application

8. What are the drawbacks of Distributed ledger?

9. Discuss the various pros and cons of Distributed ledger.

10. Write the Differences between Centralized and Distributed Ledger

11. What is Distributed Ledger Technology? How is it works?

12. Explain the step by step Working Mechanism of Blockchain architecture

Chapter – 4

ARCHITECTURAL COMPONENTS OF BLOCKCHAIN TECHNOLOGY

The implementation of blockchain varies depending on the specific use case, as different types of blockchain are better suited for different purposes. This chapter has described the common architecture of blockchain applications. This chapter also covers primary categories of blockchain networks or types of blockchain, like public blockchains, private blockchains, consortium blockchains, and hybrid blockchains. Chapter includes their advantages, disadvantages, and optimal applications.

Architectural Components of Blockchain Technology

In any blockchain application, smart contracts and consensus mechanisms are two important components (the symbolic presentation and connection between smart contracts and consensus mechanisms is shown in figure 4.1). We can say the robustness of any blockchain application is dependent upon the understanding between smart contracts and consensus mechanisms.

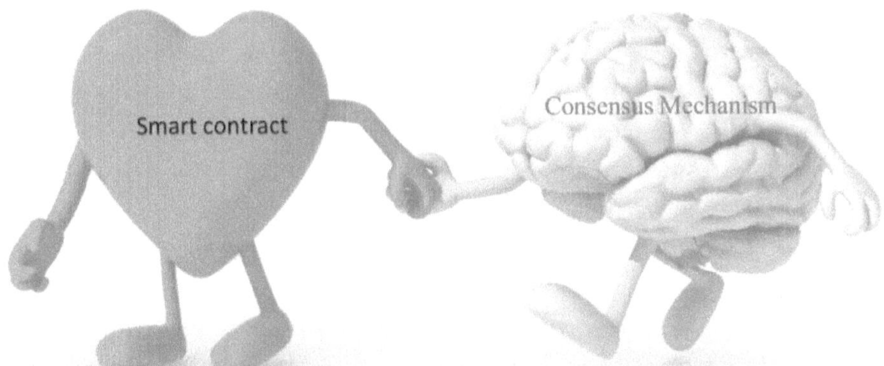

Figure 4.1: Symbolic Presentation of Smart Contract and Consensus Mechanism

In any application of blockchain technology, the role of the smart contract is to develop trust between the nodes, and the effectiveness of the decision-making process or acceptance of working mechanisms depends on consensus mechanisms. In terms of technological language, whose, how, and when the transactions are initiated in peer-to-peer networks or blockchain networks could be mentioned in smart contracts, and whose, how, and when the transactions are validated could be part of the consensus mechanism.

4.1 Smart Contract

The concept of smart contracts has existed since the 1980s, according to Szabo. However, the most significant limitation at the time was the lack of a mechanism to eliminate middlemen. Nick Szabo's whitepaper on smart contracts was first published in 1996. The utilization of blockchain technology enables the elimination of middlemen, although the establishment of trust and fulfilment of commitments among participating entities sometimes necessitates the implementation of a smart contract. The smart contract, like traditional contracts, is a set of organizational terms and conditions that govern the trust between the parties engaged within the boundaries of the contract. The main distinction is that a smart contract is written in a programming language. Controlled coding is used to apply the rules, terms, and conditions, which reflect the actual agreement agreed by all parties, or we can say, smart contracts are computer programs that execute when certain predetermined conditions are satisfied and are then recorded on a blockchain. Usually, they are employed to automate the execution of an agreement, ensuring that all parties can have immediate confidence in the outcome, without relying on a third-party. Additionally, it defines the commercial circumstances and laws that influence the time period of a transaction. In other words, smart contract software encapsulates the business logic that will be executed when certain criteria are satisfied and runs on top of the blockchain shown in figure 3. Smart contracts provide efficiency, trustworthiness, and accuracy for all parties. Simply put, smart contracts operate by executing straightforward "if/when…then…" statements that are encoded into blockchain-based code. A network of computers carries out actions once specific conditions have been met and verified. The flow of smart contact is shown in figure 4.1.

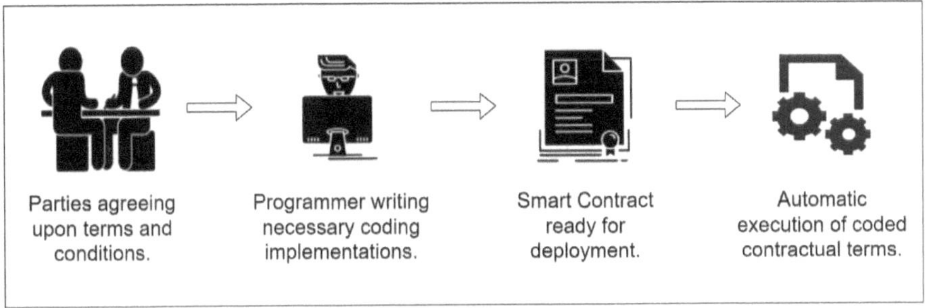

Figure 4.2: Smart Contract Workflow

One of the major advantages of using a smart contract in a blockchain application is its immutability. Once a smart contract is deployed on a blockchain network, it becomes immutable and cannot be changed or updated. However, modifications can be made if and only if all parties involved agree to accept the modified version of the smart contract. Advantages of smart contracts in any blockchain application shown in 3.2

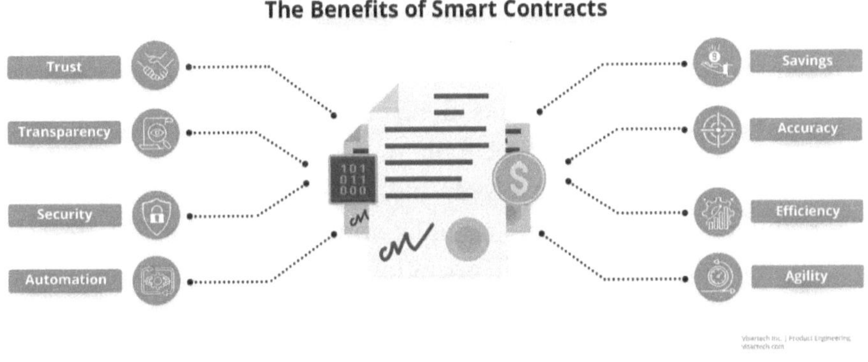

Figure 4.3: Benefits of Smart Contracts

4.1.1 Key Benefits of Creating Smart Contracts for Businesses

a) Automation is one of the benefits of smart contracts. Smart contracts offer more than automation. Smart contracts offer more features and functions:

b) Trust and Transparency: Once the contract is deployed, neither party is allowed to alter the terms of the agreement in order to obtain personal advantages. Furthermore, all terms are transparent to all parties involved, allowing for easy tracking of contract execution and access to information regarding the transaction.

c) Security: Each record is linked to the previous and subsequent records. This implies that hackers must reconstruct the entire sequence in order to alter a single ledger record. Additionally, while records are accessible to anyone, the anonymity of the parties is maintained. The parties' identities and other private information are kept confidential.

d) Automation: On the other hand, standard contracts acknowledge the potential for either or both parties to engage in dishonest behavior, disregard certain aspects of the agreement, interpret and execute the terms differently, or even fail to fulfill their obligations altogether.

e) Automation makes it impossible here. There is no need for any middleman since all the work is done mechanically. Furthermore, since all operations are managed by software, there are no occurrences of falsified data or violations of any contractual obligations.

f) Reduced Expenses: Because of automation and encryption, business owners can significantly cut down on operational costs. According to Accenture, investment banks alone could save $8 billion per year by adopting smart contract technology. All transactions are completely visible to all parties involved, and no multiple intermediaries are required to conduct and monitor complicated payments. Instead, anyone can streamline all operations in real time by themselves. Consequently, there are no fees, charges, or commissions to pay.

g) Accuracy, Efficiency, and Agility: Automation accelerates the execution of all necessary tasks. By utilizing programming, the contract's performance is guaranteed, resulting in increased accuracy for you. Once the prerequisites are fulfilled, the necessary action is carried out consistently, regardless of the individuals involved in the transaction.

4.2 Consensus Mechanism

Consensus refers to the process of reaching a unanimous decision among all participants in a network. For example, a group of friends decides to have a pizza party without any conflicts. Reaching a decision to have a pizza party together requires consensus or mutual agreement. Perhaps someone would prefer to have a dinner party instead. How can a group of friends effectively come to a consensus? Furthermore, how can many individuals who are unfamiliar with each other come to a mutual agreement within a network? To mitigate issues related to centralization and intra-group disputes, the system needs the implementation of a consensus process or algorithm. A consensus algorithm refers to a mechanism employed to maintain synchronization among network participants within a democratic framework. Decentralization entails endowing every participant within a network with equitable authority to participate in decision-making processes inside the system shown in figure 4. Therefore, it is imperative to set regulations for network participants, commonly referred to as nodes, in order to enforce system modifications through a universally accepted consensus. All-player agreement on game norms is a very prevalent example of consensus mechanisms in action.

Figure 4.4: Consensus Mechanism

There are several consensus mechanisms used in blockchain as shown in figure 4.4, including proof of work, proof of stake, delegate proof of stake, proof of authority, proof of history, and proof of burn, among others. The utilization of consensus mechanisms varies depending on the specific situations, environments, and applications. Various consensus mechanisms are explained in Chapter 5.

4.3 Layered Blockchain Architecture

As previously mentioned in Chapter 1, blockchain technology is a one-of-a-kind combination of various existing technologies such as computer networks, DBMS, cryptography, network security, and so on. Various technologies play an important role in building robust blockchain applications at different levels. The layered architecture of blockchain consists of six layers, as described in Figure 4.5.

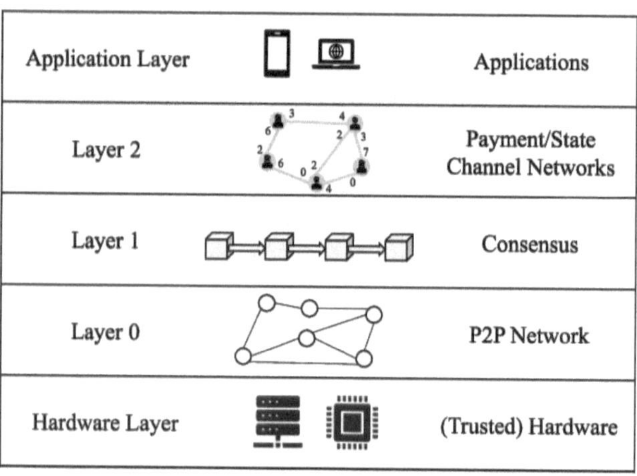

Figure 4.5: Layred Blockchain Architecture

4.3.1 Hardware Infrastructure Layer

The initial layer is referred to as the hardware layer, encompassing conventional computers, Application-Specific Integrated Circuits (ASICs), or trusted hardware. The nodes, which are interconnected within a worldwide peer-to-peer (P2P) communication network, function on the hardware infrastructure. This layer is referred to as layer 0.

4.3.2 Layer 0 (P2P network)

The nodes, which are interconnected in a worldwide peer-to-peer (P2P) communication network, function on top of the hardware infrastructure. This layer is referred to as layer 0, also known as the propagation layer. This P2P layer makes sure that nodes may connect to one another, communicate, share, and synchronize to maintain the integrity of the blockchain network. The major characteristics of peer-to-peer (P2P) are mentioned below:

a) Peers participate as equals in a network.

b) Unlike the client-server model, where there are different responsibilities: webserver compared to client-browser

c) Original Internet, Usenet

d) P2P systems share resources, storage, files, bandwidth, etc.

e) A huge number of nodes participating in the network

f) Having resources to share

g) With demands for resources they do not have

h) Peer-to-Peer (P2P) as solution

P2P offers mechanisms to find or look up what I want. Therefore: Build an additional overlay network. After finding the node providing the desired service Communicate directly from peer to peer.

4.3.2.1 Overlay Network

The concept of overlay networks is described in figure 4.6. The P2P overlay network is comprised of all the peers that are participating, with each peer acting as a network node.

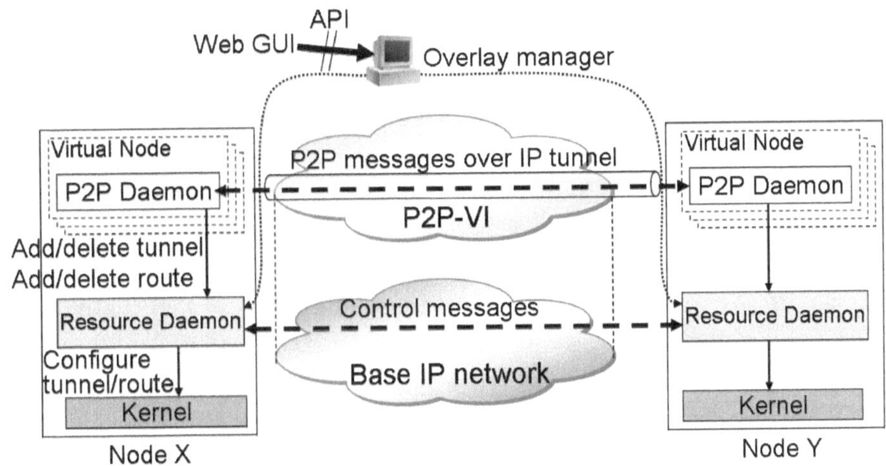

Figure 4.6: Overlay Network

In the overlay network, there is a directed edge between two nodes if they know each other. This means that if a participating peer in the P2P network knows the location of another peer, a link is established between them. P2P networks can be classified as either unstructured or structured based on the way the nodes in the overlay network are linked to each other.

a)   Unstructured Overlay Network

An unstructured P2P network is created when overlay links between nodes are established randomly. These networks are simple to build, as a new peer can join by copying the existing links of another node and gradually forming its own connections. In this type of network, when a peer needs to locate specific data, the query is broadcasted across the network to reach as many peers as possible that may have the desired data.

b)   Structure Overlay Network

Structured P2P networks address the limitations of unstructured networks by using a Distributed Hash Table (DHT), where each peer is assigned responsibility for specific content in the network. These networks rely on hash functions to assign values to both content and peers, following a global protocol to determine which peer is responsible for storing and managing particular content.

- peers and objects have identifiers, strict topology

- objects are stored on peers according to their ID

- ID: responsibleFor(ObjID) = PeerID

Let's consider an example where there are 50 nodes connected in a P2P network. Suppose that peer X is looking for a specific piece of data. In the unstructured overlay, all 49 nodes have the ability to share the desired piece of data. In the worst-case scenario, none of the nodes are sharing the data. Conversely, in the best-case scenario, all 49 nodes are sharing the desired data. On average, approximately 24 nodes are sharing the desired data. In every situation, various issues arise. In a structured overlay network, we create a single spatial data structure. This data structure contains information about the requester of a specific piece of data and the sender who is providing that data. Since this spatial data structure is accessible to all nodes, the sender's information will circulate to others, ensuring that no other node will repeatedly share the same data.

4.3.3 Layer 1 (Consensus)

The consensus layer is essential for the functioning of blockchain platforms. Remember that the blockchain serves as a distributed ledger for transactions. The term blockchain originates from the concept that chunks of transactions (blocks) are interconnected to create a chain. Every node starts with an identical copy of the initial block, referred to as the "genesis block." It is essential to reach a consensus to guarantee that once certain transactions are produced by a node, they will ultimately be incorporated into everyone's ledger, provided they adhere to the standards that each node evaluates before adding the transaction to their own historical record. The consensus layer serves as a fundamental and vital element of any blockchain. The consensus layer plays a crucial role in validating blocks, arranging them in a designated sequence, and guaranteeing unanimous agreement among all participants.

4.3.4 Layer 2 and Application Layer

The application layer includes smart contracts, chain codes, and decentralized applications (DApps). We divide the application layer protocols into two categories: the execution layer and the application layer protocols. The application layer consists of the programs utilized by end users to communicate with the blockchain network. It includes scripts, application programming interfaces (APIs), user interfaces, and frameworks. The blockchain network is the backend technology for these applications, with which they communicate via APIs. As part of the execution layer, smart contracts, underlying principles, and chaincode are all present.

4.4 Application Archiecture

Blockchain mining process is well defined in chapter 2. Step by step Application flow diagram described in figure 4.7.

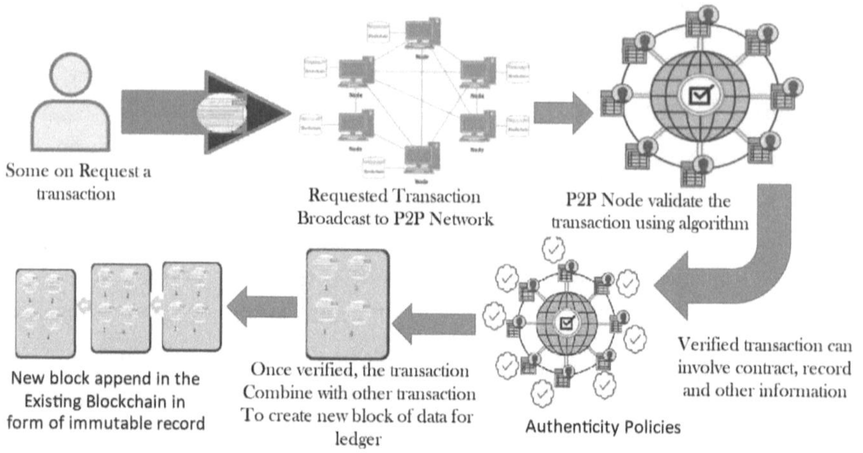

Figure 4.7: Step by step application flow diagram

The application architecture approach is quite similar to the Blockchain mining process. Any peer (user/node) can initiate the transaction to the peer-to-peer network. Once a transaction has been posted on the blockchain network, the future of that transaction is determined by the consensus process. It may be approved and added to the block, or it may be denied.

4.5 Types of Blockchain

We define blockchain as a securely shared ledger of decentralized data. Blockchain technology enables a collective group of select participants to share data. Blockchain cloud services facilitate the easy collection, integration, and sharing of transactional data from multiple sources. Cryptographic hashes serve as unique identifiers, breaking up data into shared blocks. Blockchain provides data integrity with a single source of truth, increasing security. A blockchain system prevents fraud and data tampering by requiring the permission of a quorum of the parties to alter data. You can share a blockchain ledger, but you cannot alter it. All participants will receive alerts and know who attempted to alter data.

Types of blockchains can be characterized as permissionless, permissioned, or both.

4.5.1 Permissionless Blockchain

A permissionless blockchain is a decentralized network in which anyone can participate without prior authority or consent. These blockchains allow users to join the network, validate transactions, and maintain the distributed ledger. Bitcoin and Ethereum are well-known examples of permissionless blockchains, in which participants maintain anonymity while achieving consensus through mechanisms such as proof of work (PoW) or proof of stake (PoS).

a)   Characteristics

i)   Open Access: Anyone can join, participate, and communicate with the network without prior approval. This enables users to view, write, and validate transactions freely.

ii)   Decentralization: No central authority controlling the network. Instead, all nodes in the system have equal rights, contributing to decision-making and validation.

iii)   Transparency: All transactions are publicly accessible, promoting openness and trust among participants.

iv)   Anonymity/Pseudonymity: Users can interact without showing their original identity, as permissionless networks often don't require personal identification, relying on cryptographic addresses.

v)   Consensus Mechanism: Use Proof of Work (PoW) or Proof of Stake (PoS) consensus algorithms to ensure agreement among nodes, making it difficult for any single entity to control the network.

vi)   Immutability: A permissionless blockchain provides strong guarantees of data integrity and immutability by making it nearly impossible to alter once recorded.

vii)   Incentivization: Native tokens or cryptocurrency rewards frequently incentivize participants, such as miners or validators, for their contributions to the network's security and upkeep.

b) Advantages

i)   Everyone can join (No censorship); the only need is top-notch hardware and internet.

ii) Encourage users' or entities' trust (promoting trust and accountability using Transparency).

iii) Its bigger network guarantees a great degree of transparency (Open Participation).

iv) Greater decentralizing of access helps more people (Global access or Global reach).

c)   Disadvantages

i)   Permissionless blockchains often face scalability challenges due to their consensus mechanisms, such as Proof of Work, which can result in slow transaction processing and limited capacity.

ii) Pseudonymity can be advantageous, but because it dissociates participants' identities from their actions, it also makes illicit activities like money laundering, fraud, and other criminal behavior possible.

iii) Without a centralized authority, network improvements or upgrades can cause conflicts within the community, resulting in "forks," in which the blockchain breaks into two distinct chains.

iv) Reduced privacy since many aspects are exposed.

4.5.2 Permissioned Blockchain

Only approved entities can access and participate in a permissioned blockchain, a type of decentralized network. This contrasts with permissionless blockchains, where anyone can participate. Only a specific group can validate transactions or data in these closed networks. Networks that require high privacy and security often utilize them. Enterprise environments often prioritize privacy, security, and compliance, utilizing these blockchains. The system still uses cryptographic principles but offers more control over who can interact with the network. Examples include Hyperledger Fabric and Corda.

a) Characteristics

i) Access Control: Organizations can control who can read, write, and validate transactions by restricting network participation to authorized users.

ii) Governance: A known group of participants typically governs the network, often with predefined rules for managing and overseeing operations.

iii) Privacy: Permissioned blockchains offer enhanced privacy since only approved members have access to data, making them ideal for organizations that need confidentiality in transactions.

iv) Efficiency: Due to the controlled number of participants and lower consensus overhead, permissioned blockchains are often faster and more efficient than permissionless ones in terms of transaction throughput.

v) Consensus Mechanism: For trusted environments with fewer nodes, the consensus process is more flexible and frequently employs mechanisms like Practical Byzantine Fault Tolerance (PBFT).

b) Advantages

i) This blockchain tends to be faster as it has some nodes for validations.

ii) They can offer customizability.

iii) Strong Privacy as permission is needed for accessing transaction information.

iv) As few nodes are involved performance and scalability are increased.

c) Disadvantages

i) Not truly decentralized as it requires permission

ii) Risk of corruption as only a few participants are involved.

iii) Anytime owner and operator can change the rules as per their need.

4.6 Blockchain Classification

Blockchain is classified based on their uses. Manly classified into four types: public blockchains, private blockchains, consortium blockchains, and hybrid blockchains shown in figure 4.8.

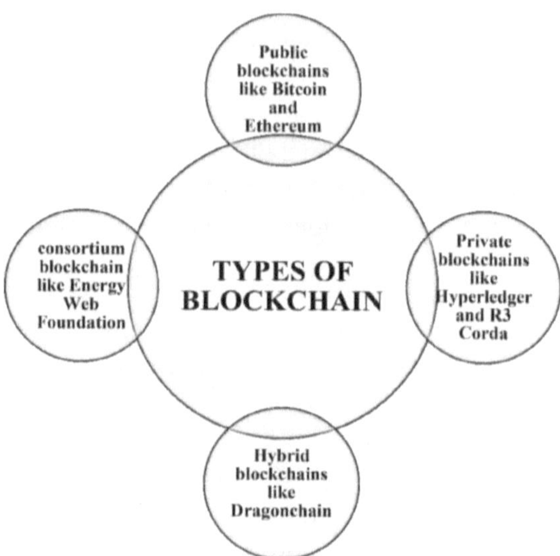

Figure 4.8: Various Blockchains

Each of these blockchain systems has advantages, disadvantages, and perfect applications. Transacting in a safe network is the fundamental use of the blockchain. For this reason, various applications of blockchain and ledger technologies exist. To guard against unwanted access to private information, multichain can be set up. It can only be accessed by authorized entities within the organization and is not accessible to the public. Which type an organization needs to choose for its job depends on that organization.

	Blockchain type		
	Public	Private	Consortium
Permissionless?	Yes	No	No
Who can read?	Anyone	Invited users only	Depends
Who can write?	Anyone	Approved participants	Approved participants
Ownership	Nobody	Single entity	Multiple entities
Participants known?	No	Yes	Yes
Transaction speed	Slow	Fast	Fast

4.6.1 Public Blockchain

Blockchain technology combines cryptography, data management, networking, and incentive systems to make it easier to verify, execute, and record transactions between parties. Every party in the network has the same copy of the distributed ledger (complete chain publicly available), and the majority will reject any tampered or altered versions. This openness is consistent with the notion of decentralization, which allows anybody with a computer and internet access to join in the network without limitation.

i)   Since this is public blockchain, anyone can access it, meaning no one owns it.

ii) Anyone who has internet access and a computer with good hardware can participate in this public blockchain.

iii) All the computers in the network hold similar copies of blocks.

iv) In this public blockchain, any node/user can also perform verification of transactions or records.

Figure 4.9 Public Blockchain

a)   Public Blockchain Features:

i)   High Security: It is secure. Due to mining (51% rule).

ii)   Open Environment: The public blockchain is accessible to everyone.

iii) Anonymous Nature: Public blockchain is ensured anonymity. There is no need to use your real name or real identity; therefore, everything would stay hidden, and no one can track you based on that.

iv) No Regulations: The public blockchain does not have any regulations that the nodes have to follow. So, there is no limit to how one can use this platform for their betterment.

v) Full Transparency: Public blockchains allow you to see the ledger anytime you want. There is no scope for corruption or discrepancies, and everyone has to maintain the ledger and participate in consensus.

vi) True Decentralization: This type of blockchain operates without the presence of a central entity. Thus, the responsibility of maintaining the network is solely on the nodes. They are updating the ledger, which promotes fairness with the help of a consensus algorithm.

vii) Full User Empowerment: Typically, in any network, a user has to follow a lot of rules and regulations. In many cases, the rules might not even be fair. But not in public blockchain networks. Here, all of the users are empowered, as there is no central authority to look over their every move.

viii) Immutable: When something is written to the blockchain, it cannot be changed.

ix) Distributed: Unlike a client-server approach, the database is not centralized, and all nodes in the blockchain participate in the transaction validation.

b)   Advantages

i) Trusted: There are algorithms in place to detect no fraud. Participants need not worry about the other nodes in the network.

ii) Secure: This blockchain boasts a large size due to its open nature. A large size allows for a greater distribution of records.

iii) Anonymous Nature: It is a secure platform that allows you to conduct transactions properly, without requiring you to reveal your name or identity in order to participate.

iv) Decentralized: The network is not maintained by a single platform; instead, each user maintains a copy of the ledger

c) Disadvantages

i) Processing: Due to the large size of the network, transaction processing occurs at a slow pace. Verifying each node is a time-intensive task.

ii) Energy Consumption: The proof-of-work mechanism requires substantial energy consumption and demands powerful computer hardware to participate in the network.

iii) Acceptance: Without a central authority, governments face challenges in adopting and implementing the technology more rapidly.

d) Use Cases

Proof of work or proof of stake mechanisms secure public blockchains, which have the potential to disrupt traditional financial systems. A key innovation within public blockchains is the smart contract, which enhances their ability to support decentralized operations. Examples of public blockchains include cryptocurrency and Ethereum. Public blockchains provide a variety of financial services, including lending, borrowing, and trading, without the need for traditional banks.

Public blockchains are permissionless in nature, allow anyone to join, and are completely decentralized. Public blockchains allow all nodes of the blockchain to have equal rights to access the blockchain, create new blocks of data, and validate blocks of data.

4.6.2 Private Blockchain

In a private blockchain, there is a participant who has exclusive control over the rules governing the blockchain. private blockchains function similarly to public blockchains by using peer-to-peer connections and maintaining some degree of decentralization, they typically operate on a smaller scale i.e. It operates within a restricted environment, such as a closed network or under the management shown in figure 4.10, which enhances their security compared to fully open networks. These blockchains are not as decentralized as the public blockchain only selected nodes can participate in the process, making it more secure than the others.

i) These systems are not as transparent as a public blockchain.

ii) Only authorized users can access them.

iii) A closed network operates these blockchains. In this way, few people are allowed to participate in a network within a company/organization.

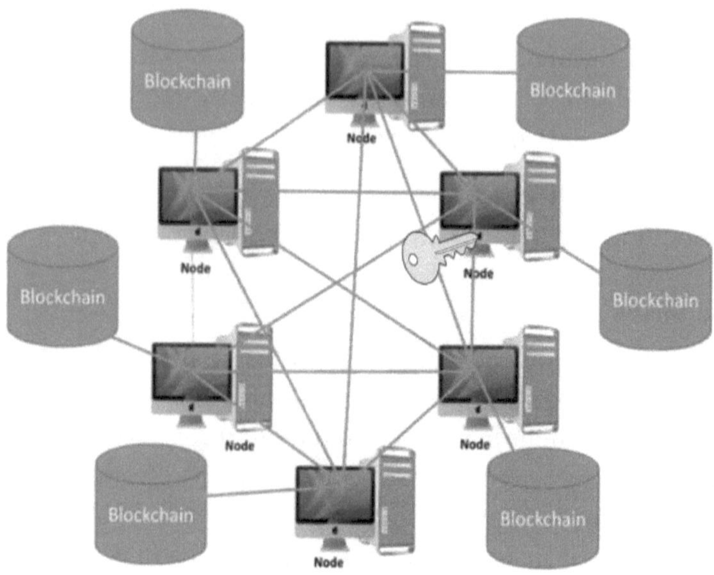

Figure 4.10: Private Blockchain

a) Features of Private Blockchain

i) Full Privacy: This approach primarily addresses privacy concerns. Private blockchains are more centralized.

ii) High Efficiency and Faster Transactions: When the nodes are distributed locally and there are fewer nodes participating in the ledger, the performance is faster.

iii) Better Scalability: Being able to add nodes and services on demand can provide a great advantage to the enterprise.

b) Advantages

i) Speed: The smaller size of the network expedites transaction processing and reduces the time required for node verification.

ii) Scalability: You can manually customize the network size by adjusting the scalability.

iii) Privacy: Businesses have enhanced privacy measures to ensure confidentiality within the network.

iv) Balanced: By limiting access to transactions to a select group of users, the network achieves greater balance and enhances overall performance.

c) Disadvantages

i) Security: With fewer nodes, the possibility of manipulation rises, making these blockchains more vulnerable.

ii) Centralized: One important disadvantage is trust-building, as the centralized structure can lead to potential violations by companies.

iii) Node Count: The small number of nodes means that if several go offline, the entire blockchain system could be at risk.

d) Use Cases

Proper security and maintenance make this blockchain a great asset for securing information without exposing it to the public eye. Therefore, companies use them for internal auditing, voting, and asset management. An example of private blockchains is Hyperledger and Corda. Here are some key use cases of private blockchains:

i) Supply Chain Management: Private blockchains can enhance transparency and traceability in supply chains by allowing authorized parties to track goods and verify data throughout the production and delivery process.

ii) Finance and Banking: Private blockchains can streamline interbank transactions, settlements, and cross-border payments while maintaining confidentiality. They offer improved security, faster processing, and reduced operational costs.

iii) Healthcare: Private blockchains enable secure sharing of patient records and medical data between authorized parties, ensuring data integrity and privacy and reducing administrative inefficiencies.

iv) Enterprise Resource Planning (ERP): Businesses can use private blockchains to automate and optimize internal processes such as procurement, inventory management, and auditing, ensuring transparency within the organization.

v) Digital Identity Verification: Private blockchains can store and verify personal identities, providing secure and controlled access to identity information for organizations like banks, government agencies, and healthcare providers.

vi) Voting Systems: Organizations can use private blockchains for secure, transparent, and tamper-proof voting, ensuring that only authorized participants can cast ballots and preventing fraud.

vii) Real Estate: Private blockchains can manage property transactions, ownership records, and legal contracts securely, reducing fraud and increasing the efficiency of property transfers.

vii) Intellectual Property and Licensing: Private blockchains can manage digital rights and intellectual property, ensuring that only authorized parties have access to specific content or licenses with a clear record of ownership and usage rights.

These use cases demonstrate how private blockchains can improve security, efficiency, and transparency in various industries.

 *Private blockchains are like public blockchains; only they are managed by one central authority. This authority decides who is allowed to participate in the network, verify transactions and maintain the shared ledger. Therefore, these networks are only partially decentralised as public access to these blockchains is restricted.*

4.5.3 Hybrid Blockchain

Hybrid blockchains include aspects of both private and public blockchains, making them appealing to businesses that want the best of both worlds. As mentioned in figures 4.11(a) and 4.11(b), it allows businesses to construct a separate, permissioned system alongside the public, permissionless system, granting them control over which blockchain data becomes public and which remains private. Some organizations control certain parts of the private and public blockchain, while others are visible on the public blockchain. It is a combination of both public and private blockchains.

i) Systems that are permission-based as well as permissionless are utilized.

ii) Smart contracts provide users with the ability to access information.

iii) In the case of a hybrid blockchain, even a principal entity is unable to make any changes to the transaction

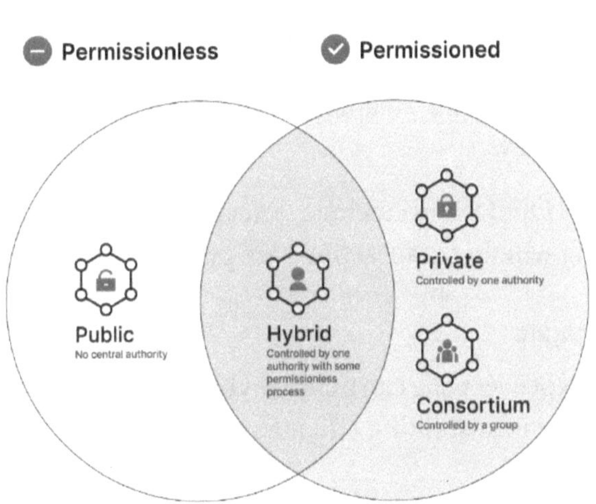

Figure 4.11 (a): Hybrid Blockchain

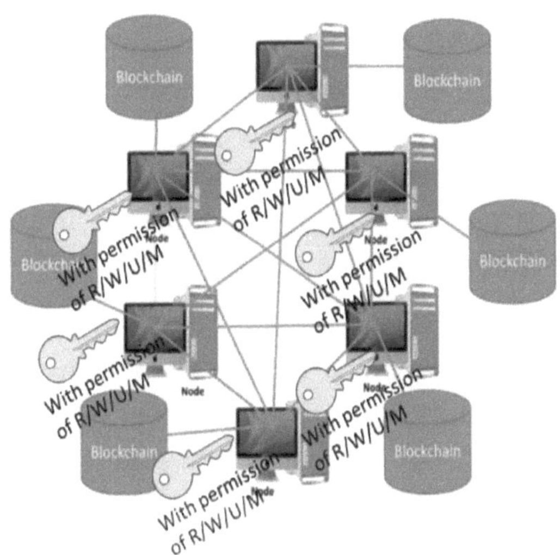

4.11 (b): Working Mechanism of Hybrid Blockchain

a) Advantages

i)   Ecosystem: The most significant feature of this blockchain is its hybrid nature. Because 51% of users do not have access to the network, minimum venerability.

ii) Cost: Transactions are affordable since they only require verification from a few nodes. Because not all nodes perform the verification, the computational cost is decreased.

iii) Architecture: It is highly adaptable while yet ensuring integrity, security, and transparency.

iv) Operations: Operations include selecting blockchain members and determining whether transactions are publicly available.

b) Disadvantages

i)   Efficiency: Not everyone can build a hybrid blockchain. The corporation also has issues in sustaining efficiency.

ii) Transparency: Users may be unaware of hidden facts. If a user asks access via a hybrid blockchain, the organization has the option to approve or reject access.

iii) Ecosystem: The blockchain's closed ecosystem does not provide incentives for network membership.

c) Use Case

It offers a comprehensive solution to the health care industry, government, real estate, and financial companies. Hybrid Blockchain offers a solution for public data access while ensuring private protection. Examples of hybrid blockchain are ripple networks and XRP tokens.

i)   Supply Chain Management: Hybrid blockchains enable companies to safeguard sensitive data, such as pricing or supplier agreements, on the private side, while simultaneously offering transparency and traceability to the public regarding product origin or shipment tracking. This combination ensures accountability while protecting proprietary information.

ii)   Government and Public Services: Hybrid blockchains can be used by governments to securely manage sensitive data on the private side, such as citizen records or tax information, while giving transparency on the public side, such as voting systems, land registrations, or budget spending.

iii) Internet of Things (IoT): In IoT applications, hybrid blockchains can manage private data from devices (for example, usage data or sensitive sensor information) on the private side while sharing essential data on a public blockchain to ensure compliance, traceability, and accountability during device interactions.

The term "hybrid blockchain" is commonly used to describe a blockchain that combines elements of both public and private blockchains. This blockchain is under the control of a single corporation, enabling organisations to construct private, permission-based systems alongside public, permissionless systems.

4.5.4 Consortium Base Blockchain

A consortium blockchain refers to a combination of several private blockchains owned by many organizations. Figure 4.12 illustrates how each organization functions as a node on the blockchain, representing a stakeholder within the consortium. The stakeholders grant authorization to join or exit the network. Each organization within the consortium has the ability to administer their own node or blockchain, enabling them to access, share, and distribute the data contained inside.

Consortium blockchains encourage collaboration among complementing blockchains. This method allows individuals to solve their own problems and create consortium-wide solutions. It is a creative approach that solves the needs of the organization. This blockchain validates the transaction and also initiates or receives transactions.

i)   Sometimes referred to as the Federated Blockchain.

ii)   The needs of the company can be satisfied through the utilization of this creative approach. Some of the sections are open to the public, while others are off-limits to the public.

iii) When it comes to this particular form of blockchain, it is managed by different entities.

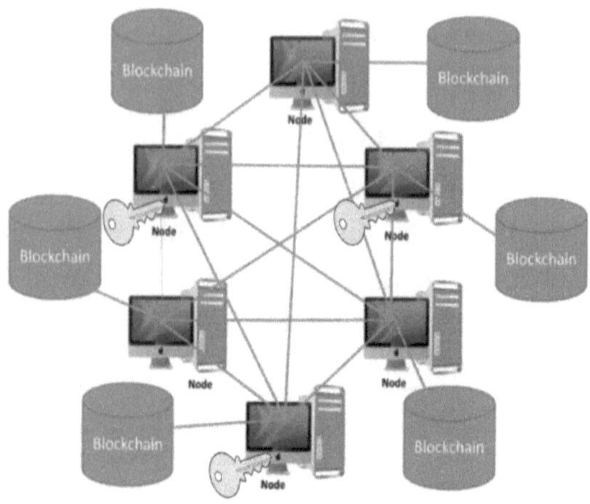

Figure 4.11 (a): Hybrid Blockchain Mechanism

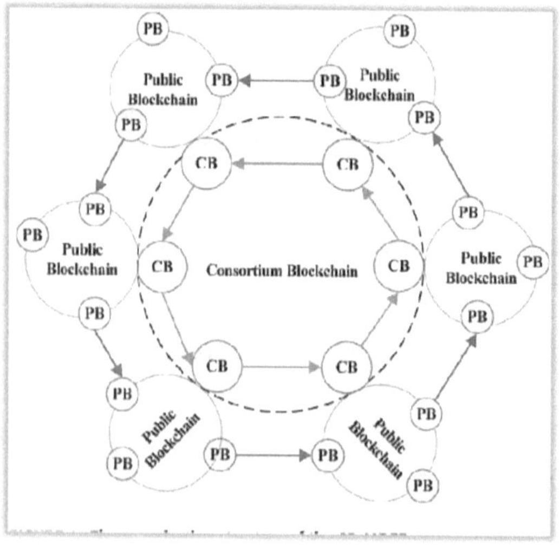

Figure 4.11 (b): Workflow diagram of Hybrid Blockchain

a) Advantages

i) **Shared Control:** A group of organizations rather than a single entity governs consortium blockchains. Multiple parties distribute decisions and governance, fostering trust and reducing the risk of centralization.

ii) **Enhanced Security:** Compared to public blockchains, the network is more secure against malicious attacks because only a specific group of authorized participants can access the blockchain. Only trusted parties can validate transactions, reducing the likelihood of fraud or tampering.

iii) **Scalability**: Consortium blockchains offer better scalability than public blockchains. With a limited number of nodes involved in transaction validation, the network can process transactions more quickly and efficiently.

iv) **Privacy:** Consortium blockchains offer enhanced privacy by restricting the sharing of sensitive data to authorized members of the consortium. This makes them ideal for industries like finance, healthcare, and supply chain, where privacy is crucial.

v) **Faster Consensus:** Since only selected, trusted nodes participate in the consensus process, reaching agreement on transactions is faster and more efficient than in public blockchains, leading to quicker transaction finalization.

b) **Disadvantages**

i) **Partial Decentralization:** Consortium blockchains offer a greater degree of decentralization compared to private blockchains; however, they do not achieve the complete decentralization characteristic of public blockchains. A limited number of members hold concentrated control, which may result in power imbalances and collusion among participants.

ii) **Trust Concerns:** Even though consortium blockchains consist of various organizations, there remains a necessity for participants to have a certain level of trust in one another. When a small group of members takes control of decision-making, it may erode the trust of other participants and result in conflicts.

iii) **Complex Governance:** Achieving consensus in a consortium blockchain presents challenges due to the participation of various organizations that may have differing interests. Creating a transparent and equitable governance framework can be a lengthy and challenging process.

iv) **Consortium blockchains:** designed for approved participants only, provide less transparency than public blockchains, where the ledger is accessible to all. This absence of transparency could diminish trust from outside parties or the general public.

v) **Reduced Participation:** Consortium blockchains limit involvement to chosen entities, which means they miss out on the advantages of the extensive, decentralized networks found in public blockchains. This restricts the creativity and variety of concepts that arise from greater community engagement.

The complexity of initial setup lies in the need for cooperation and coordination among various organizations when establishing a consortium blockchain. It entails the establishment of consensus rules, governance models, and technology integration, which can be intricate and require significant time investment.

The term "consortium blockchain" refers to a group of private blockchains, each owned by individual institutions that have banded together to share information to improve existing workflows, transparency and accountability.

Test your skill

1. Discuss the various Architectural components of Blockchain Technology.

2. Explain the Smart Contract in detail.

3. List out the Key Benefits of Smart Contracts for Businesses

4. What is consensuses mechanism?

5. Discuss the Layred Blockchain Architecture in detail.

6. Write the major characteristics of Peer-to-Peer (P2P).

7. What is overlay.

8. Discuss the unstructured and unstructured overlay.

9. Explain the Application flow diagram (Application Archiecture) blockchain technology.

10. Discuss the characteristics of permissionless and permissioned blockchain application.

11. Described the characteristics of public blockchain technology. Write it advantages and disadvantages.

12. Described the characteristics of private blockchain technology. Write it advantages and disadvantages.

13. Described the characteristics of consortium blockchain technology. Write it advantages and disadvantages.

Chapter – 5

CONSENSUS ALGORITHMS

A consensus algorithm in blockchain technology facilitates agreement among multiple distributed systems or processes on a single piece of data. This chapter concentrates on consensus processes and algorithms that foster trust in decentralized environments. There are various types of consensus mechanisms, each operating on distinct principles.

5.1 Consensus Mechanism

In decentralized systems, particularly in blockchains, a consensus mechanism is a method or protocol that facilitates agreement among multiple participants (or nodes) on the network's state. Indicate the process for adding new blocks to the blockchain, as shown in Figure 5.1. In the context of blockchain technology, which involves the storage, maintenance, and distribution of recorded data over a decentralized network of computers, it is required to provide a system for resolving disputes that may emerge among the network members.

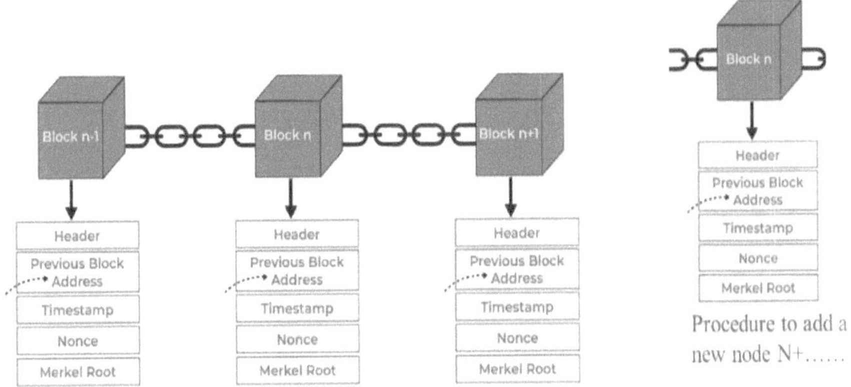

Figure 5.1: Procedure to add new block (Need Consensus)

Consensus Mechanism

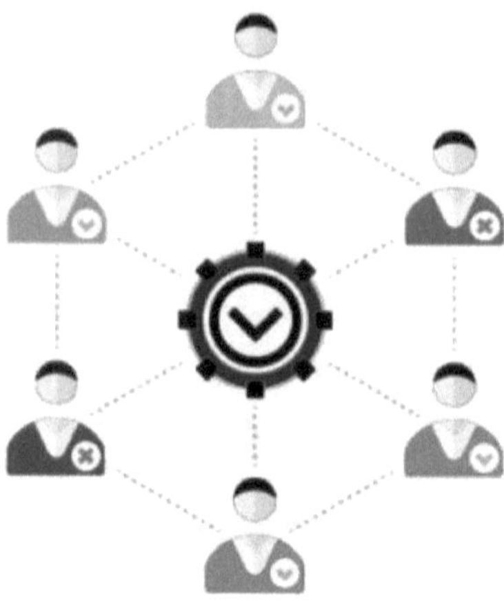

Figure 5.2: Agreement (Consensus)

Consensus mechanisms (Figure 5.2)—that is, self-regulating stacks of software protocols created into blockchain code—synchronize a network to agree on the status of a digital ledger, thus verifying criteria are used to validate every transaction within a blockchain. As Figure 5.3 shows, blockchain systems can be essentially separated into three layers: the network layer, the consensus layer, and the incentives layer.

Incentives Layer

(Incentive model, rewarded elements (e.g., blocks and transactions), amounts of rewards, reward distribution, ...)

Consensus Layer

(Consensus protocol (e.g., PoW, PoS etc), transactions execution, block generation and reception, fork resolution, ...)

Network Layer

(Nodes, network configurations, information to be propagated (e.g., transactions and blocks), P2P broadcast protocol, ...)

Figure 5.3: Blockchain System Layers.

The network layer of a blockchain system describes the network nodes, their physical locations, and their connections. The consensus layer of a blockchain system specifies the algorithms and rules that nodes must follow in order to come to a consensus on the state of the blockchain. The rules dictate the frequency of block creation, the number of copies of the ledger each node can retain, and the authorization of nodes to generate and contribute the next block to the blockchain. Blocks and transactions in a blockchain system typically have their own accompanying incentives, known as block rewards and transaction fees, respectively.

 *Blockchains contain software algorithms called consensus mechanisms that enable networks agree on the status of digital ledgers. Programming a network's verification standard involves consensus methods. Each method prevents fraudsters from tampering with the record.*

There are various types of consensus mechanism, each of which works on different principles.

5.2 Byzantine Fault Tolerance

Barbara Liskov and Miguel Castro introduced the first consensus algorithm, Byzantine Fault Tolerance, in the late 90s. Derived from the Byzantine Generals' Problem, it employs collective decision-making to safeguard against system failures, thereby reducing the influence of faulty nodes, even when some nodes fail or respond incorrectly. To put it simply, the Byzantine Generals Problem is a game theory problem that illustrates the challenges faced by decentralized parties in reaching a consensus without depending on a trusted central party. In a network where no member can confirm the identity of other members, how can participants collectively reach a consensus on a specific truth? Figures 5.3 (a), 5.3 (b), 5.3 (c), and 5.3 (d) explain four different cases to better understand the Byzantine Generals' Problem., and 5.3 (d).

Case 1:	
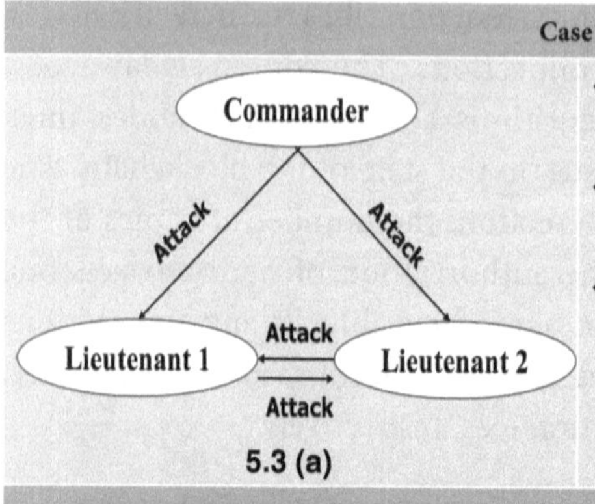 	• No Malicious Node/ Faulty Node/ Agent Node • All are working very Smoothly as per plan • Outcome: Attack (No logical dilemma

Case 2:	
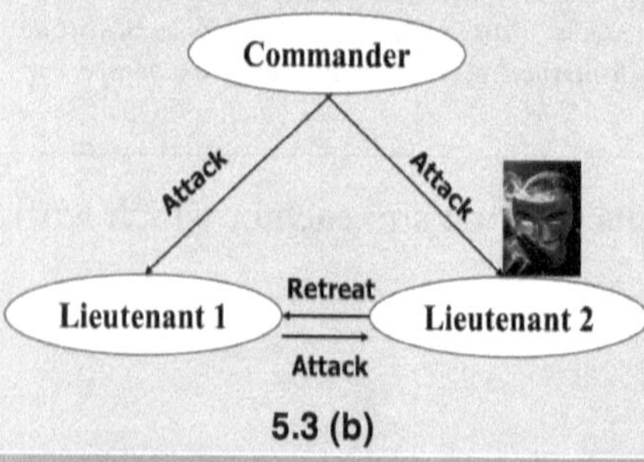 	• Lieutenant 2 is either Malicious Node/ Faulty Node/ Agent Node • Not going well, something and somewhere is problem. • Stage: Lieutenant 1 is in logical dilemma • Outcome: Lieutenant 1 can be attack or retreat

Case 3:	
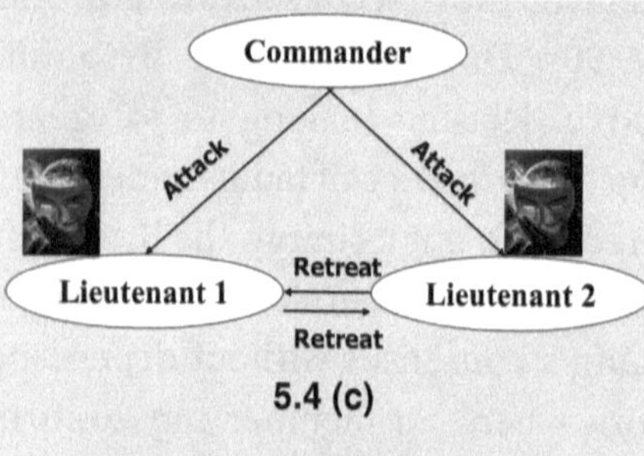 	• Lieutenant 1 and Lieutenant 2 both are either Malicious Node/ Faulty Node/ Agent Node • Not going well, something and somewhere is problem. • Stage: Lieutenant 1 and Lieutenant 2 both is in logical dilemma • Outcome: Lieutenant 1 and Lieutenant 2 can be attack or retreat.

Case 4:	
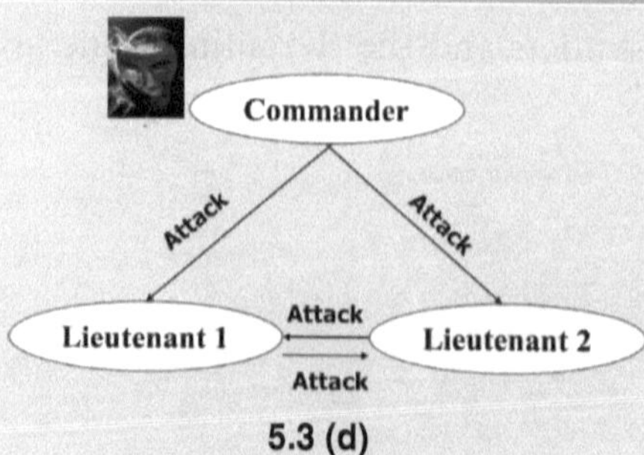 	• Commander is either Malicious Node/ Faulty Node/ Agent Node • Not going well, something and somewhere is problem. • Stage: No logical dilemma • Outcome: attack

The Byzantine Fault Tolerance refers to the capability of a computer system to keep functioning even in the presence of node failures or malicious actions. The term originates from a hypothetical scenario known as the Byzantine Generals Problem. This logical dilemma, as you'd expect, is about a group of Byzantine generals. Each general has an army and a position surrounding a fortress, and they must collectively decide whether to attack or retreat. If they all make the same decision, they're successful. However, if a miscommunication or treachery leads some generals to attack while the others retreat, the battle becomes lost. These types of problems are known as Byzantine faults, shown in figure 5.3. We can regard each individual node in a computer system comprising multiple nodes as a general node. The system's Byzantine fault tolerance refers to whether it can keep working even when some nodes go down or intentionally try to deceive it. Byzantine Fault Tolerance has importance from a computing standpoint because it indicates that a system can continue to operate even if specific components fail. An aircraft or space probe, both of which utilize computing systems, must possess the capability to function even when not all of their modules are operating at 100% capacity. The Byzantine Generals' Problem forms the basis of BFT. Byzantine Fault Tolerance (BFT) is a feature of a distributed network that enables consensus (agreement on the same value) even when some nodes in the network fail to respond or respond with incorrect information. The objective of a BFT mechanism is to safeguard against system failures by employing collective decision-making (both correct and faulty nodes), which aims to reduce the influence of the faulty nodes.

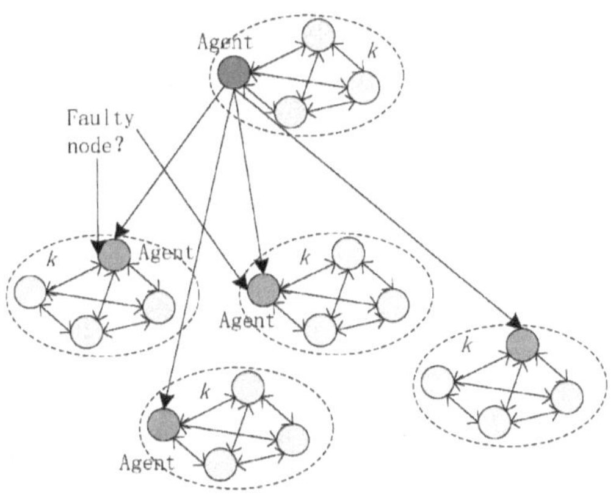

Figure 5.5: Byzantine Fault Tolerance

We can achieve byzantine fault tolerance if the correctly functioning nodes in the network agree on their values. We may assign a default vote value to a message if we do not receive it within a predetermined period of time, leading us to believe that the message originated from a specific node and was therefore "faulty." If the majority of nodes provide a valid response, we may also provide a default response. Leslie Lamport demonstrated that if we have 3m+1 correctly functioning processors, we can establish consensus (agreement on the same state) if at most m of them are flawed, which means that strictly speaking, more than two-thirds of the total number of processors should be trustworthy.

5.2.1 Types of Byzantine Failures:

We consider two categories of failures. One is fail-stop (in which the node fails and stops operating), and the other is arbitrary-node failure. Below are a few examples of arbitrary node failures.

a) Failure to return a result

b) Respond with an incorrect result.

c) Respond with a deliberately misleading result.

d) Respond with a different result to different parts of the system.

5.3 Practical Byzantine Fault Tolerance (pBFT)

Practical Byzantine Fault Tolerance (pBFT) is a system that has a primary node and secondary nodes. These nodes work together to reach a consensus, making this system one of the solutions to the Byzantine Generals Problem. We design the pBFT function to function efficiently in asynchronous systems, where the response time to a request has no upper limit. We optimize it to achieve low overhead time. The goal of this system was to address numerous issues related to the existing Byzantine fault tolerance solutions. Application areas include distributed computing and blockchain. Major advantages of pBFT include:

i) **Energy Efficiency**: pBFT can achieve distributed consensus without carrying out complex mathematical computations (like in PoW).

ii) **Transaction finality:** Once finalized and agreed upon, the transactions do not require multiple confirmations, unlike the PoW mechanism in Bitcoin, where every node individually verifies all the transactions before adding the new block to the blockchain; approvals can take between 10 and 60 minutes depending upon how many entities confirm the new block.

iii) **Low Reward Variance:** Because every node in the network participates in responding to client requests, it is possible to incentivize every node, which results in low reward variance for nodes that aid in decision-making.

Figures 5.4 (a) and 5.4 (b) demonstrate how pBFT attempts to provide a practical Byzantine state machine replication that can function even when malicious nodes are operating in the system.

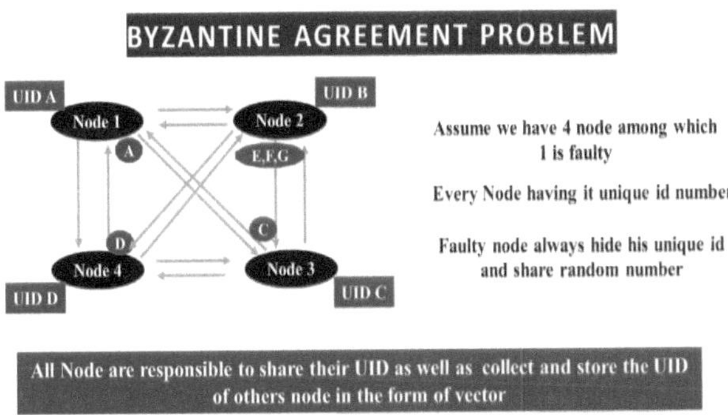

Figure 5.4 (a): Solution Byzantine agreement Problem

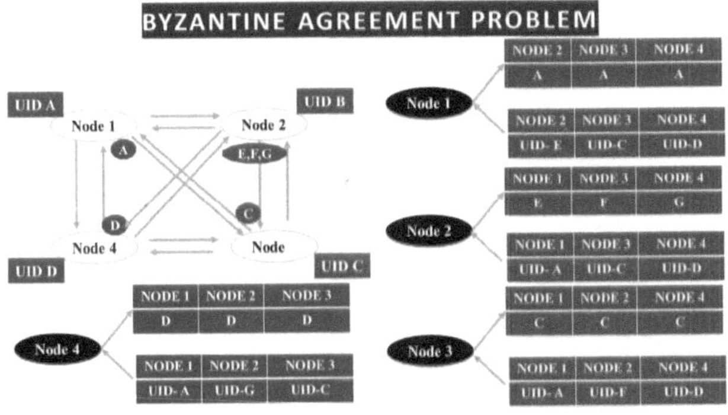

NODE 2	NODE 3	NODE 4
A	A	A

NODE 2	NODE 3	NODE 4
UID-E	UID-C	UID-D

NODE 1	NODE 3	NODE 4
E	F	G

NODE 1	NODE 3	NODE 4
UID-A	UID-C	UID-D

NODE 1	NODE 2	NODE 4
C	C	C

NODE 1	NODE 2	NODE 4
UID-A	UID-F	UID-D

NODE 1	NODE 2	NODE 3
D	D	D

NODE 1	NODE 2	NODE 3
UID-A	UID-G	UID-C

Figure 5.4 (b): Solution Byzantine agreement Problem

A decentralization system or consensus mechanism, known as Practical Byzantine Fault Tolerance (pBFT), possesses a property that enables consensus among distributed nodes, even in the presence of faulty or malicious nodes. Up to one-third of the nodes in a pBFT system can exhibit Byzantine behavior, which allows them to act arbitrarily or dishonestly. A pBFT system can also handle network delays, partitions, or failures without compromising the consensus. A pBFT-enabled distributed system sequentially orders its nodes, designating one as the primary (or the leader node) and the others as secondary (or the backup nodes). Note here that any eligible node in the system can become primary by transitioning from secondary to primary (typically in the case of a primary node failure). The goal is for all honest nodes to help reach a consensus regarding the state of the system using the majority rule. Zilliqa – pBFT in combination with PoW consensus, Hyperledger Fabric – permissioned version of pBFT, Tendermint – pBFT + DPoS(Delegated Proof-of-Stake) are common Platforms using pBFT variants.

RBFT – Redundant BFT, ABsTRACTs, Q/U, HQ – Hybrid Quorum Protocol for BFT, Adapt Zyzzyva – Speculative Byzantine Fault Tolerance, Aardvark are another platforms to enhance the quality and performance of pBFT for specific use cases.

We divide pBFT consensus rounds into four phases:

First: The client sends a request to the primary (leader) node.

Second: The primary (leader) node broadcasts the request to all the secondary (backup) nodes.

Third: The primary and secondary nodes carry out the requested service before responding to the client.

Forth: The request is served successfully when the client receives'm+1' replies from different nodes in the network with the same result, where m is the maximum number of faulty nodes allowed.

Every view (pBFT consensus rounds) changes the primary (leader) node, and if a predefined amount of time passes without the leading node broadcasting a request to the backups (secondary), a view change protocol can substitute the primary. If needed, a majority of the honest nodes can vote on the legitimacy of the current leading node and replace it with the next leading node in line.

a)   Limitations of pBFT:

The pBFT consensus model is effective only in small numbers of nodes in the distributed network since the significant communication overhead increases exponentially with every additional node.

i)   Sybil Attacks: The pBFT systems allow one entity (party) to manage several identities, hence enabling Sybil attacks. As the number of nodes in the network increases, Sybil attacks become increasingly difficult to carry out. However, because pBFT mechanisms also face scalability issues, they often work in conjunction with other mechanisms.

ii)   Scaling: pBFT does not scale well because of its communication overhead (with all the other nodes at every step). As the number of nodes in the network increases (it increases by $O(n^k)$, where n is the message and k are the number of nodes), so does the time taken to respond to the request.

iii)   Network Synchrony Requirements: pBFT presupposes a partially synchronous network, where message delays are inevitable but not always predictable. Network partitions or excessive delays may hinder the achievement of consensus, thereby impacting performance and reliability, as partial synchrony is crucial.

Byzantine Fault Tolerance (BFT) is a crucial feature in computing systems, allowing a system to continue functioning even when certain components fail. It is derived from Byzantine Generals' Problem and aims to safeguard against system failures by employing collective decision-making, reducing the influence of faulty nodes, even when some nodes fail or respond incorrectly.

5.4 Proof of Work (PoW)

Proof of Work (PoW) is the first approach applied by a blockchain network to achieve consensus. The most popular cryptocurrency networks, such as Bitcoin and Litecoin, or public blockchains, use Proof of Work (PoW) as a common consensus algorithm. A participant node must demonstrate that their submitted work qualifies them to add new transactions to the blockchain. This approach verifies the transaction and appends a new block to the chain. In this method, a group of individuals known as "miners" engage in competition to complete the network transaction. Mining is a competitive process where individuals or entities vie against one another. Upon successfully creating a valid block, miners receive immediate rewards. People widely recognize Bitcoin as the most well-known application of Proof of Work (PoW). Today, most cryptocurrencies use Proof of Work consensus as their preferred consensus mechanism. Markus Jakobsson and Ari Juels coined the phrase "Proof of Work" for the first time in a publication in 1999. The purpose of a consensus mechanism is to bring all the nodes in agreement—that is, to trust one another—in an environment where the nodes don't trust each other.

To understand the proof of work, first we have to understand "Who can add the block to the blockchain" and "What is the procedure to add the block to the blockchain? The answer to the first question is "miner," who has the ability to add a block to the blockchain. However, the definition of a miner varies depending on the type of blockchain. In a public blockchain, any node with sufficient computational power and the ability to solve the required puzzle within a specified timeframe can become a miner. However, in a private blockchain, a miner can be a member of a specific group, and all members of this group will meet the same criteria.

The second question is more important than the first: "What is the procedure for adding the block to the blockchain?" Normally, we validate all the transactions in the new block before adding it to the blockchain. Keep in mind, the chain with the longest block height will add the block. Miners, which are special computers on the network, carry out computational tasks to solve a complex mathematical problem, thereby adding the block to the network, a process known as Proof-of-Work. With time, the mathematical problem becomes more complex.

5.4.1 Working Procedure

'Proof' refers to the solution of a highly complex problem, and 'work' refers to the process of solving the same. The Proof of Work (PoW) consensus algorithm involves solving a computationally challenging puzzle in order to create new blockchain blocks. Colloquially, the process is known as mining', and the nodes in the network that engage in mining are known as miners.

Solving the "hard mathematical problem" to connect the new block to the final block in the valid blockchain uses the most energy. When a miner finally finds the right solution, the node broadcasts it to the whole network at the same time. The following steps illustrate the systematic working procedure:

Step 1: In a blockchain application, the block structure is the same for all nodes, as illustrated in figure 5.5(a).

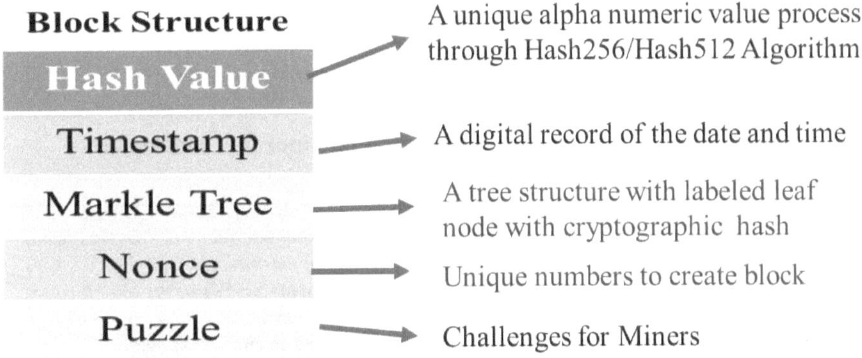

Figure 5.5 (a): Common Block Structure

a)   Block structure is common for all Miners

b)   Timestamp, Markle tree and Puzzle is known for all Miners

c)   Miners have to calculate unique Nonce or solve the Puzzle and get unique answer

Step 2: The miners, also known as nodes, will solve the puzzle, identify the unique nonce, and then calculate the hash value of block

Step 3: Miner will check the difficulty level; if Hash (Block) > Difficulty Level, then Miner will broadcast the nonce in the decentralized or distributed network shown in figure 5.4 (b).

Step 4: All other nodes or participants will once again calculate the hash value of the block using a shared nonce and confirm the difficulty level, thereby completing the verification process. We will then add the block to the blockchain and increase the difficulty level accordingly.

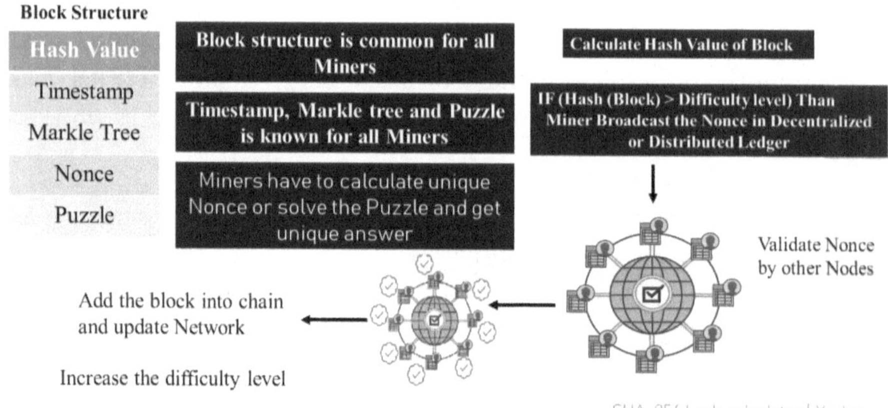

Figure 5.5 (b): Step by step process to add block into blockchain

Proof of work (PoW) is a blockchain consensus mechanism that requires significant computing effort from a network of devices. The concept was adapted from digital tokens by Hal Finney in 2004 through the idea of "reusable proof of work" using the 160-bit secure hash algorithm 1 (SHA-1). Proof of work (PoW) is a decentralized consensus mechanism that requires network members to expend effort in solving an encryption puzzle.

5.4.2 Bitcoins Proof of Work System:

Bitcoin utilizes the Hash Cash Proof of Work system as its mining foundation. Given data A, find a number x such that the hash of x appended to A results in a number less than B. The miners bundle up a group of transactions into a block and attempt to mine it. To mine it, one must solve a challenging mathematical problem. We refer to this problem as the proof of work problem, which requires a solution to demonstrate the miner's effort in solving the problem and, consequently, the validity of the mined block.

For the solution to receive approval, the target hash must be less than the block's hash. The header of a hashed block must equal or be less than the target hash in order to send a new block and reward to a miner. Block generation is more challenging the lower the aim is. A miner keeps trying various unique values, or "nonces," until one comes up that works. The miner who successfully solves the problem receives the bitcoin reward and broadcasts the block's addition to the blockchain. The target hash adjusts once every 16 blocks, or approximately every 2 weeks. All the miners immediately stop working on the block and start mining the next block. There are two main features that have contributed to the wide popularity of this consensus protocol. First, it is hard to find a solution to the mathematical problem; second, it is easy to verify the correctness of that solution.

Bitcoin introduced the most widely used proof-of-work consensus, SHA-256. Others include Scrypt, SHA-3, Scrypt-jane, Scrypt-n, etc.

5.4.3 Major issues with Proof-of-Work consensus:

There are several issues with the Proof-of-Work consensus mechanism.

i) 51% risk: If a controlling entity owns 51% or more than 51% of nodes in the network, the entity can corrupt the blockchain by gaining the majority of the network.

ii) Time-consuming: Miners must examine numerous nonce values to determine the correct answer to the puzzle required to mine the block, a task that takes a significant amount of time.

iii) Resource consumption: Miners consume high amounts of computing power in order to find the solution to the challenging mathematical puzzle. It leads to the waste of valuable resources (money, energy, space, and hardware).

iv) Transaction confirmation takes significantly more time. Therefore, the transaction is not instantaneous, as it requires some time to mine, add, and commit to the blockchain.

5.4 Proof of Stack (PoS)

Proof of Stake (PoS) is a type of algorithm that aims to achieve distributed consensus in a blockchain. Quantum mechanics first proposed this method of consensus, and Sunny King and his colleagues later published a paper on it. This led to Proof-of-Stake (PoS)-based Peercoin. A stake is a value or monetary bet on a specific outcome. The process is called staking.

Before proof of stake, the most popular way to achieve distributed consensus was through proof-of-work (implemented in Bitcoin). However, proof-of-work requires a significant amount of energy, specifically electricity, when mining Bitcoin. So, a proof-of-work-based consensus mechanism increases an entity's chances of mining a new block if it has more computation resources. Apart from the aforementioned points, a PoW-based consensus mechanism has additional weaknesses that we will address in a later section. In such a scenario, a proof-of-stake-based mechanism holds merit. As the name suggests, nodes on a network stake a certain amount of cryptocurrency to become candidates for validating new blocks and earning fees. Then, an algorithm chooses, from the pool of candidates, the node that will validate the new block. This selection algorithm combines the quantity of stake (amount of cryptocurrency) with other factors (like coin-age-based selection, randomization process) to make the selection fair to everyone on the network.

a) Coinage-based selection: The algorithm tracks the duration of each validator candidate node's validity. The likelihood that a node will replace a validator increases with age.

b) Random block selection: We select the validator using a combination of "lowest hash value" and "highest stake." The new validator is the node with the best weighted combination of these.

Ethereum (ETH), Cardano (ADA), Polkadot, Tezos, and Algorand are blockchain platforms that have adopted Proof of Stake (PoS). Regular Proof-of-Stake, Delegated Proof-of-Stake, Leased Proof-of-Stake, and Master Node Proof-of-Stake are different versions of PoS.

A typical PoS-based mechanism workflow:

1. Nodes make transactions. The PoS algorithm puts all these transactions in a pool.

2. All the nodes competing to become validators for the next block raise a stake. We combine this stake with other factors like 'coin-age' or 'randomized block selection' to select the validator.

3. The validator verifies all the transactions and publishes the block. He has not yet received the forging reward, and his stake remains locked. This is to allow the nodes on the network to approve the new block.

4. If the block is 'OK', the validator gets the stake back and the reward too. If the algorithm employs a coin-age-based mechanism for validator selection, it resets the coin-age of the validator for the current block to 0. This resets his coin-age to 0, making him a low priority for the next validator election.

The algorithm marks the validator as 'bad' and loses its stake if other nodes on the network fail to verify the block. The process begins anew at step 1 to forge the new block.

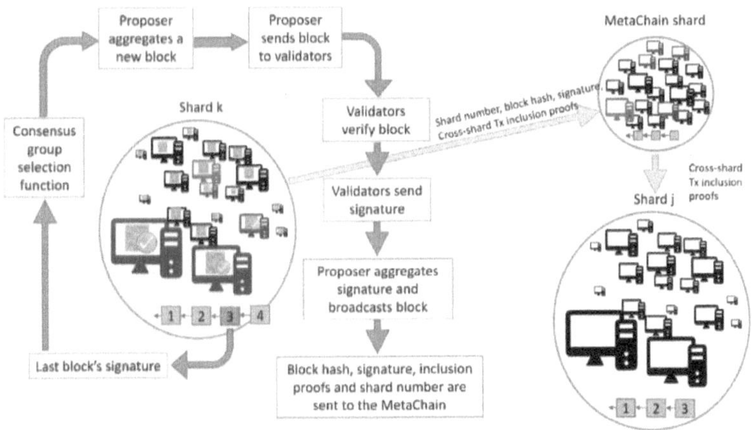

Figure 5.6: Proof of Stake

5.4.1 Proof of Stake Advantages

Here are the key features of Proof of Stake:

a) There are only a limited number of coins available on the network at any given time. The network does not have the ability to create new coins. Note that the network begins with a finite number of coins in proof of stake (PoS).

b) Every transaction incurs a fee, which serves as a reward for minters and forgers. The entity that forges the new block receives this accumulated amount. Note that if the forged block is found fraudulent, the transaction fee is not rewarded. Additionally, the validator loses their stake, a process known as slashing.

c) In Proof-of-Stake (PoS) technology, the network's security is based on economic incentives. Since validators must lock up a significant amount of cryptocurrency or coins to participate, they have a strong financial incentive to behave honestly. If they act maliciously, they risk losing their stakes.

d) The 51% attack is impractical because the attacker must own 51% of the network's cryptocurrency, which is expensive. This makes the attack extremely tedious, costly, and not very profitable. When collecting such a large share of cryptocurrency, there may not be enough currency to buy, and buying more coins/value will become more expensive. Additionally, if the validator validates incorrect transactions, they will lose their stake, resulting in a negative reward.

e) PoS has the potential to be more scalable than PoW because it doesn't require constant competition among miners. Without the high resource consumption and delays from block mining, PoS can allow for faster block times and higher transaction throughput. (More scalable than PoW.)

f) The lack of competition among nodes to add new blocks to the blockchain leads to energy savings, making it energy efficient.

g) Decentralization: In blockchains such as Bitcoin, which use a Proof of Work system to achieve distributed consensus, there is an additional incentive in the form of exponential rewards to join a mining pool, resulting in a more centralized nature of the network. In the case of a proof-of-stake-based system (like Peercoin), rewards are proportional (linear) to the amount of stake. Therefore, it offers no additional incentive to participate in a mining pool, thereby fostering decentralization.

h) Security: A person attempting to attack a network will have to own 51% of the stakes (pretty expensive). This leads to a secure network.

5.4.2 Challenges in PoS Proof of Stake:

Proof of Stake (PoS) offers several advantages over Proof of Work (PoW), such as energy efficiency and scalability. However, for a secure and functional system, we must carefully address the unique challenges and potential vulnerabilities it presents. Here are some of the main challenges associated with PoS:

a) In PoS, validators do not incur significant costs for supporting multiple conflicting chains, unlike in PoW, where mining on two chains would require splitting computational resources. This could encourage validators to sign multiple blocks at the same height, potentially leading to chain splits and forks.

b) In Proof of Stake (PoS), a participant's chances of selecting to validate the next block and earn rewards increase with the number of tokens they stake. Over time, this can result in a situation where a few large validators control a significant portion of the network, a phenomenon known as delegation centralization.

c) Some PoS systems incorporate penalties for collusion and misbehavior but detecting and preventing it can still be challenging. We also use distributed validator sets and governance mechanisms to enhance decentralization and diminish the likelihood of collusion.

d) PoS necessitates "weak subjectivity," which implies that nodes cannot independently verify the chain without relying on trusted information, like checkpoints or trusted peers. This differs from PoW, where nodes can independently verify the longest chain based on computational power alone.

Proof of Stake (PoS) is an algorithm for achieving distributed consensus in a Blockchain, first proposed by Quantum Mechanic and later developed by Sunny King and his peers. It is based on the concept of staking, where nodes stake a certain amount of cryptocurrency to become candidates for a new block. This selection algorithm combines stake quantity with factors like coin-age and randomization to ensure fairness for all network members.

5.5 Proof of Authority (PoA)

We can divide blockchain platforms' consensus mechanisms into permissionless (like Ethereum, Bitcoin) and permissioned (like Hyperledger,

Ethereum Private). A permissioned blockchain pre-selects all nodes, unlike a permissionless blockchain where anyone can become a node. This enables the use of consensus types that offer high scalability and bandwidth. One of these consensus types is **proof-of-authority (PoA) consensus,** which provides high performance and fault tolerance. Gavin Wood, the co-founder of Ethereum and Parity Technologies, proposed the term in 2017.

5.5.1 PoA Mechanism

In PoA, give the priority to generate new blocks to nodes that have proven their authority. We refer to these nodes as "validators," and they operate software that enables them to include transactions in blocks. The automated process does not necessitate constant computer monitoring from validators, but it does require them to maintain uncompromised computers. Both private networks and public networks, such as the POA Network, can benefit from PoA, as it distributes trust. The PoA consensus algorithm leverages the value of identities, which means that block validators are not staking coins but their own reputation instead. The PoA is secured by trust in the selected identities, much like in the KYC or document verification processes. PoA is not decentralized but aims to improve centralized systems. PoA validators are visible to anyone. Knowing the identities of validators could potentially lead to manipulation by third parties.

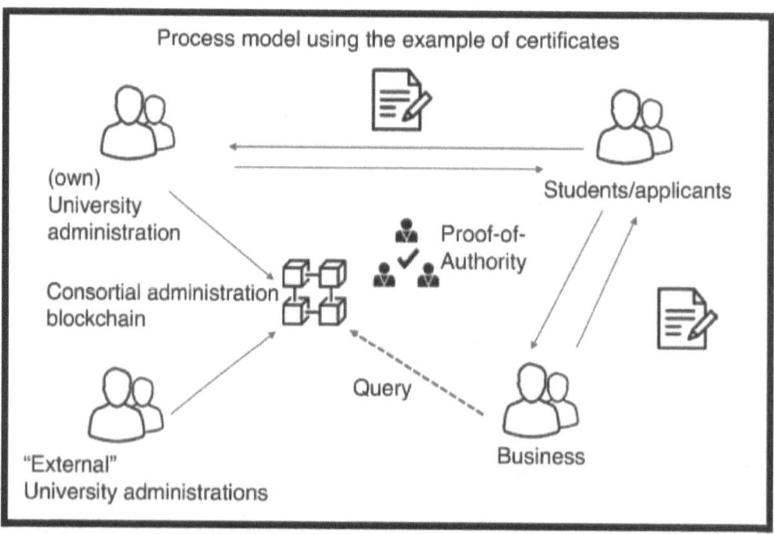

Figure 5.3: Proof of Authority

The major conditions associated with proof of authority are firstly validators need to confirm their real identities, second a candidate must be willing to invest money and put his reputation at stake. Third, A hard process of selecting validators and incentivize long-term commitment to the blockchain. Fourth, Method for selecting validators must be maintain integrity of blockchain. Some sort of process should be there to select honest validators. The major application areas of PoA are private and consortium blockchains, government and public sector, enterprise-level applications, and digital rights management.

5.5.2 Security Attacks in PoA Consensus

a) A Distributed Denial of Service (DDoS) attack is an attempt to make an online service unavailable by overwhelming it with traffic from multiple sources. An attacker sends a large number of transactions and blocks to a targeted network node in an attempt to disrupt its operation and make it unavailable. The PoA mechanism enables defence against this attack by pre-authenticating network nodes and granting block generation rights only to those nodes capable of withstanding DoS attacks.

b) In PoW consensus, 51% attack requires an attacker to obtain control over 51% of network nodes. Obtaining control of the nodes in a permissioned blockchain network is much harder than obtaining computational power. PoA gives nodes the opportunity to become validators, which motivates them to maintain their positions. Reputation serves as an incentive for validators, enabling them to maintain their authority as a node. PoA only permits non-consecutive block approval from a single validator, thereby centralizing the risk of serious damage to the authority node.

Proof-of-Authority (PoA) consensus, proposed in 2017 by Ethereum co-founder Gavin Wood, offers high performance and fault tolerance. It awards blocks to validators who have proven their authority, requiring uncompromised computers. PoA is suitable for private and public networks, leveraging the value of identities and ensuring trust on selected identities.

5.6 Proof of Burn (PoB)

An Another consensus method aiming at solving the high energy consumption problem of a PoW system is proof of burn (PoB). It operates on the principle of allowing miners to "burn" virtual currency tokens. The system then grants miners the right to write blocks in proportion to the coins they have burned. A miner burns their coins to acquire a computerized mining apparatus that enables them to mine blocks. As the miner burns more coins, the size of their virtual mining "rig" increases. The miners send the coins to a verifiably unascendable address before burning them. This operation solely utilizes the burned coins, ensuring the network remains responsive and active. Depending on the implementation, miners can burn either the local currency or the alternative currency. In exchange, they receive a reward in the native currency token on the blockchain. To keep mining capability, the PoB system has set up a mechanism encouraging the regular burning of cryptocurrency currencies. Instead of a one-time, early expenditure, this encourages consistent engagement by the miners. To maintain a competitive edge, miners may also need to periodically invest in better equipment as technology advances.

5.6.1 Working Mechanism of Proof-of-Burn

Sometimes, nodes refer to the process of burning coins as 'destroying' them, but the coins remain on the network; rather, we should conceptualize burning as an irreversible public action that transfers the coins to another address. The term "proof-of-burn" refers to locking some amount of cryptocurrencies, i.e., sending them to an non spendable address in exchange for tokens on some other blockchain. The idea behind proof-of-burn (PoB) is that it creates a "negative mining" incentive. In other words, to create new tokens, someone must first destroy some existing ones. Blockchain projects often utilize proof-of-burn to safeguard their tokens from devaluation. A standard proof-of-burn scheme generates and uses a public key to send cryptocurrencies or tokens. The public key allows users to generate and examine the amount of "virtual cryptocurrencies" burned at any given time.

5.6.2 Advantages of Proof-of-Burn

The proof-of-burn (PoB) consensus process has several benefits. The main advantages are as follows:

a) It offers more security and resistance to censorship, i.e., much more difficult to censor transactions or block nodes participating in the network.

b) It reduced energy consumption, i.e., more environmentally friendly.

c) No centralization issues.

d) Fair distribution of currency, i.e., it helps to prevent the distribution of new coins only to those who are willing to put their resources toward the network.

5.6.3 Disadvantages of Proof-of-Burn

a) The proof-of-burn (PoB) consensus process has several issues. The main isues are as follows:

b) Initial investments are very high, i.e., One of the most common challenges is, required significant investment to join the network.

c) It is against the decentralized concept; Proof-of-Burn goes against this by controlling those who hold the most coins.

d) Risk of speculation; a potential issue with PoB is that it could be used for speculation, therefore it could lead to instability.

Proof of Burn (PoB) is an alternative consensus algorithm that addresses energy consumption issues in PoW systems. It allows miners to "burn" virtual currency tokens, allowing them to write blocks proportional to the coins burned. Burnt coins are like mining rigs, increasing the size of the miner's virtual mining apparatus. The system rewards miners with native currency tokens in exchange for burning local or alternative chains. To maintain mining power, the system promotes periodic burning of coins, reducing power each time a new block is mined.

5.7 Proof-of-Probability (PoP)

In Proof of Probability (PoP), probabilistic models are used to select a validator or miner to propose the next block. Factors like as the participant's previous behavior, network participation, or economic stake may impact this, but the final selection is determined by randomness or probability.

5.8 Proof-of-Importance

The Proof-of-Importance (PoI) consensus mechanism is a unique protocol for blockchain networks that aims to honor users based on their overall contribution to the network. The NEM (New Economy Movement) blockchain platform first offered it as a replacement for more traditional consensus processes like Proof-of-Work (PoW) and Proof-of-Stake (PoS). procedural activities are illustrated in figure 5.4. Important characteristics of Proof-of-Importance (PoI) include:

i)   In the PoI consensus mechanism, users' ranks are an indicator that evaluates their overall impact on the blockchain ecosystem.

ii) PoI promotes the holding capacity of cryptocurrency and transaction activity by incentivizing users who actively participate in the network.

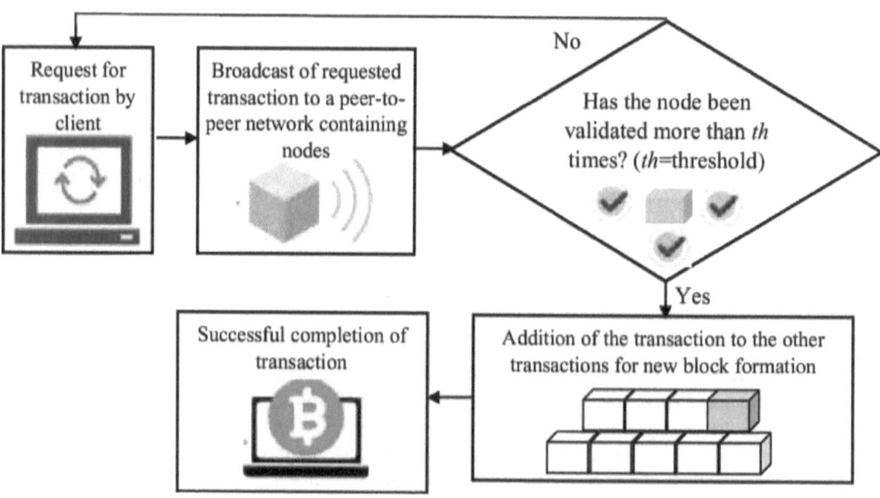

Figure 5.4: Proof of importance

5.7.1 Proof of importance Advantages

i)   Users are motivated to not only retain coins but also to actively transact and enhance the network's development.

ii) PoI is more environmentally friendly than PoW since it does not need big amounts of processing capability.

iii) PoI establishes a balance between the significance of wealth and transaction activity, in contrast to PoS, where the wealthiest stakeholders may predominate.

5.9 Proof-of-Capacity

Proof-of-Capacity (PoC), or Proof-of-Space (PoSpace), is a blockchain consensus mechanism enabling miners to utilize their available physical drive space for transaction validation and new block mining. In contrast to conventional proof-of-work (PoW), which depends on computational power, proof-of-capacity (PoC) utilizes storage capacity, resulting in greater energy efficiency. Networks such as Chia incorporate time elements to establish consensus, which is referred to as Proof-of-Space-and-Time (PoST). Working mechanism is illustrated in figure 5.5

Understanding the Basics of PoC Consensus

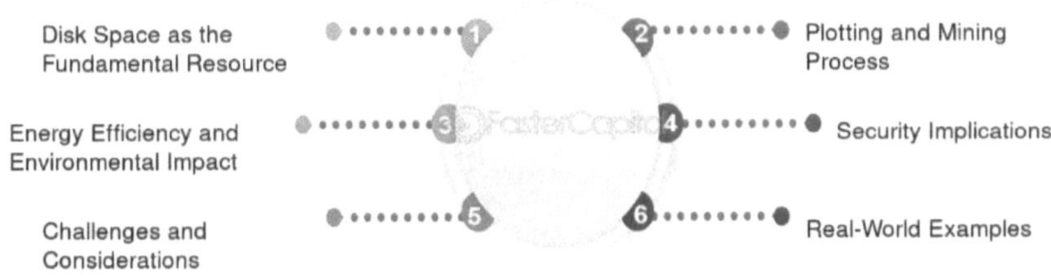

Figure: 5.7 Proof of Capacity

Prior to miners' participation, it is essential for them to map out their internal drives. Plotting entails the precomputation of possible solutions to a cryptographic puzzle, which are then stored on the drive. This step, while utilizing a considerable amount of computational resources, takes place only a single time.

After the plotting phase, the mining process gets started. The network issues a challenge to miners when it is time to mine a new block. Every miner refers to their saved data (plots) to discover a solution to the puzzle. The miner who arrives at the nearest solution to the puzzle secures the opportunity to mine the subsequent block and receive the block reward.

As miners utilize storage space instead of computational power, PoC demonstrates significantly greater energy efficiency compared to PoW. The mining competition focuses on the amount of storage a miner has dedicated to the network, rather than the processing power they can generate.

If there is a change in the cryptographic puzzle or mining algorithm, miners might have to replot their drives. This process may take considerable time, but it is typically uncommon unless there are substantial changes to the blockchain's protocol.

Test your skills

1. What do you mean by Consensus? What is role of Consensus Algorithms in blockchain applications?

2. Is Consensus Algorithms application dependent? Justify your answer.

3. Explain the concept of Byzantine Fault Tolerance.

4. How practical Byzantine Fault Tolerance solve the Byzantine Generals Problem?

5. Discuss the various Consensus Algorithms?

6. Write the advantages and disadvantages of Proof of Works Consensus Algorithms.

7. Write the advantages and disadvantages of Proof of Stake Consensus Algorithms.

8. How is the Proof of Stake Consensus Algorithms differing from Proof of Importance Consensus Algorithms?

9. Discuss the working procedure of Proof-of-Capacity.

10. Discuss Proof-of-Burn Consensus Algorithms. Write it advantages and disadvantages.

Chapter – 6

CRYPTOCURRENCY

Cryptocurrency is any digital or virtual money that uses encryption to secure transactions. Central authorities neither issue nor regulate cryptocurrencies. They use a decentralized method to record transactions and produce units. The alternative digital payment method does not require banks to authenticate transactions.

6.1 Introduction of Currency

The transfer of goods and services requires a standardized unit of measurement to determine their value. Currency serves as an intermediary and a universal standard. People use currency to exchange goods and services. People widely acknowledge government-issued paper or coins as currency. Bartering involves people exchanging products and services without money. Currency has replaced bartering as the main way to exchange goods and services.

Currency is tangible cash. In financial markets, currencies are national economies' units of account, and market variables influence their exchange rates. Business is worldwide; thus, people often require foreign cash. There are two main ways governments can handle this. Fixing the currency rate is one possibility. Governments set the exchange rate between their currencies and major global currencies like the U.S. dollar and euro. A country's central bank buys or sells pegged currency to preserve exchange rate stability. A stable exchange rate provides security, especially in nations with less developed financial institutions. Investors feel more confident when they know how much pegged currency they can buy.

Fixed exchange rates have initiated many currency crises in recent decades. When market forces prevent the central bank from maintaining the limit, this can happen. Most modern currencies are affected by market factors, with central banks acting to control severe volatility.

In India, the Reserve Bank of India (RBI) is responsible for issuing the Indian Rupee (INR) as the official currency. The most widely accepted global currencies include the U.S. dollar, the U.K. pound sterling, the euro, the Japanese yen, and the Australian dollar, among others. Some examples of other currencies include the Canadian Dollar, Chinese Yuan, Indian Rupee, Brazilian Real, Russian Rubble, and Turkish Lira.

6.2 Digital Currency

Digital currency refers to the electronic version of traditional fiat currency, which can be stored in digital wallets or withdrawn from ATMs. The currency is backed by the Reserve Bank of India, the same authority that backs the Indian currency. It can be exchanged for actual currency when it is launched in 2023. One such example is CBDC, or Central Bank Digital Currency, which is an electronic equivalent of cash and coins. In addition to cash, the public will have widespread access to this new central bank-issued money for use on a variety of devices. Digital currencies raise cybersecurity and privacy concerns.

6.3 Cryptocurrency

Cryptocurrency refers to a digital payment system that operates independently of traditional banking institutions for transaction verification. The system is designed to facilitate peer-to-peer transactions, allowing individuals from any location to easily send and receive payments. Cryptocurrency payments differ from physical money in that they are not carried around or exchanged in the real world. Instead, they exist solely as digital entries in an online database that records specific transactions. When you transfer cryptocurrency funds, the transactions are documented in a publicly accessible ledger. People store cryptocurrency in digital wallets.

We can define cryptocurrency as one type of digital currency that operates in a decentralized manner, utilizing blockchain technology and cryptography for security. In order to comprehend cryptocurrency, it is necessary to have a basic understanding of three key terms: blockchain, decentralization, and cryptography.

A cryptocurrency is a programmed data string that represents a unit of currency. Peer-to-peer networks called blockchains keep track of and manage cryptocurrency transactions like purchases, sales, and transfers. They serve as safe transaction ledgers as well. Cryptocurrencies can function as both an accounting system and a currency by utilizing encryption technology. You will learn more about cryptocurrencies and their operation in this chapter. The main differences between cryptocurrencies and digital currency are listed in Table 6.1.

Digital currency	Cryptocurrency
Digital currency is the electronics form of flat money that can be used contactless transaction	*Cryptocurrency is a store of value that is secured by cryptography.*
Digital currency is regulated by central authority (central bank)	*Cryptocurrency is decentralized and unregulated*
Digital currency rate is stable currency globally acceptable.	*Cryptocurrency rate is unstable and not globally accepted.*
Digital currency transactions are knowns as sender, receiver, and bank.	*Cryptocurrency transaction are publicly available and recorded in digital ledger.*
Digital currency needs strong password to protect digital wallet, banking app, credit and debit card.	*Cryptocurrency is secure by encryption technique.*

A cryptocurrency is a kind of virtual money that transacts securely through the use of cryptography. It functions as a medium of exchange on a computer network, independent of a central authority. Since cryptocurrencies have no regulatory authority, they use a decentralized system to record transactions and issue new units. Cryptocurrency uses blockchain technology. Mining, a process that uses computer hardware to solve complex mathematical problems, creates cryptocurrency units. There are many cryptocurrencies in the market, like Dogecoin, Bitcoin, and many more. A process known as mining creates the units of cryptocurrency. Mining is the process of validating cryptocurrency transactions and creating new units of currency. The mining process uses powerful computer hardware and software to solve complex mathematical problems that generate coins.

Blockchain technology is employed by cryptocurrencies. As a result, cryptocurrency miners, who also serve as nodes on the blockchain network where these transactions occur, endeavor to decrypt the block that contains the transaction information whenever a cryptocurrency transaction occurs. The block not only verifies the transaction but also furnishes information regarding the amount of cryptocurrency sent, the date, and the recipient. The majority of nodes in the blockchain network decrypt and approve a block as authentic, thereby incorporating it into the blockchain. In terms of the necessary computing power, the verification procedure is extremely resource-intensive. As a result, individual cryptocurrency miners often find the process too expensive, leading them to join mining pools to share computing power.

Cryptocurrency is a decentralized digital currency that uses cryptography for secure transactions, allowing it to function without a central authority. It relies on blockchain technology and involves a mining process to validate transactions and create new units. Examples include Bitcoin and Dogecoin.

6.3.1 How Does Cryptocurrency Work

Governments or central regulatory agencies do not currently govern cryptocurrencies. Indeed, most governments are actively pursuing the launch of government-regulated new cryptocurrencies. As a concept, cryptocurrency operates independently of the banking system using various brands or types of currencies, with Bitcoin being the most prominent. The blockchain is a decentralized public ledger on which cryptocurrencies operate. Currency holders maintain and update this ledger, which serves as an exhaustive record of all transactions. The mining procedure generates cryptocurrency units. This process generates currency by employing computer power to solve intricate mathematical problems. Users also have the option to purchase currencies from brokers and subsequently store and utilize them through cryptographic wallets. If you possess cryptocurrency, you do not possess any physical assets. You possess a key that enables you to transfer a record or unit of measure directly between individuals without the need for a trusted third party.

i)   "Mining" is the process that generates cryptographic currencies, which are entirely digital. It is a complex process. A "miner" solves a series of mathematical challenges using specialized software and hardware to "mine" bitcoins.

ii) Buying, selling, and storing: Today, the buying and selling of cryptocurrencies is facilitated by centralized exchanges, brokers, and private individuals. Exchanges or platforms such as Coinbase are the most convenient options for buying and selling cryptocurrency. You can store cryptocurrencies in digital wallets after purchasing them. Digital wallets can be classified into two categories: "hot" or "cold." A "hot" wallet refers to a wallet that is connected to the internet, enabling convenient transaction capabilities. However, this also increases the wallet's susceptibility to theft and fraud. On the other hand, opting to store cryptocurrency in cold storage provides a higher level of security. However, it is important to note that this approach may introduce some complexities when it comes to conducting transactions.

iii) Transacting: You can easily transfer cryptocurrencies, such as Bitcoins, from one digital wallet to another using only your smartphone. Once you own them, you have three options:

a)   Spend them on products and services.

b)   Exchange them.

c)   convert them to currency

Using a debit card-style transaction is the most convenient method for making Bitcoin purchases. You can also use these debit cards to withdraw funds, just like you would with an ATM. Using bank accounts or peer-to-peer transactions, it is feasible to convert cryptocurrencies to cash. Currently, cryptocurrencies are not governed by governments or central regulatory agencies. As a concept, cryptocurrency operates independently of the banking system using various brands or types of currencies, with Bitcoin being the most prominent.

6.3.2 Platform for Generating Cryptocurrency

Cryptocurrencies, which reside on the blockchain, are digital currencies that function identically to their traditional counterparts: they are used to purchase products and services and to receive payment for transactions. A distinguishing characteristic of cryptocurrencies over conventional ones is that they require an online network to facilitate and authenticate all transactions.

Blockchain supports all cryptocurrencies. This ensures that each transaction is thoroughly documented and transmitted over the blockchain, ensuring accountability. This prevents other parties from hacking or manipulating the digital ledger. Platform selection depends on consensus procedure. Blockchain is a digital database that permanently retains bitcoin transactions. Remember that not all transactions are considered. Blockchain consensus mechanisms provide that capability. Simply put, a consensus mechanism is a communication system that decides whether a blockchain network accepts a transaction. Several popular and flexible blockchain platforms are used to create cryptocurrencies. Some popular and flexible blockchain platforms are as follows:

1. **Ethereum:** Ethereum is the first blockchain to offer a token creation service. It offers a superior level of trust due to its maturity and strong position in the cryptocurrency market. All tokens built on Ethereum use the **ERC-20 standard.** Tokens on Ethereum can only be written in Solidity (its own programming language).

2. **EOS:** EOS tokens use the **EOSIO.** Token standard and can be created with C++ or any other language like python, java, etc. that compiles to WebAssembly. With no transaction fees, blockchains offer excellent scalability, high transactions per second, and cost-effectiveness.

3. **NEO:** Neo is an open-source community-driven blockchain platform, Neo's vision is to be an open network for a smart economy. Neo uses the NEP-5 standard. Unlike Ethereum, you can create your own tokens on it using almost any high-level programming language like Java, Python, etc. HTTP API can be used to interact with the blockchain.

4. **Cudo Miner:** Cudo Miner is a feature-oriented CPU and GPU miner that supports several algorithms. This cryptocurrency mining platform is extremely easy to set up and provides lucrative features that might not be available in other prominent mining software or platforms.

6.3.3 Create Cryptocurrency

The process of creating a cryptocurrency is illustrated in figure 6.1. The procedure for establishing a cryptocurrency is as follows:

1. Select a consensus mechanism: Decentralization is fundamental of cryptocurrencies. Cryptocurrencies depend on consensus mechanisms to verify transactions on the blockchain, ensuring the maintenance of

this decentralized structure. Consensus mechanisms are the protocols that determine the legitimacy of a transaction and facilitate its addition to the block. The two most common consensus mechanisms are proof of work (PoW) and proof of stake (PoS). Each of these methods is essential for maintaining the integrity and safety of cryptocurrency transactions. Choosing between these two consensus mechanisms is a significant decision for anyone involved in cryptocurrency development. While PoW is known for its robust security, PoS offers a more eco-friendly and sustainable option.

2. Select a Blockchain Platform: Selecting the appropriate blockchain platform for your business is contingent upon the consensus mechanism you opt for.

3. Design the Nodes: It is essential to establish the operational framework of your blockchain and modify your nodes to align with that functionality.

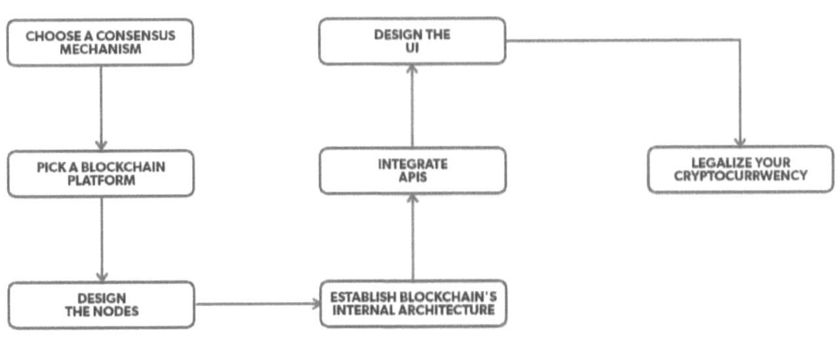

Figure 6.1: Creation of Cryptocurrency

4. Establish the Blockchain's Architecture: Ensure the internal architecture of the blockchain is well-established before its launch, as you won't have the ability to modify several parameters once it's operational.

5. Designing the UI: Building a top-notch cryptocurrency is useless if your UI is bad. Make sure the web, FTP server, and external databases

are current, and approach front-end and back-end programming with future upgrades in mind.

6. Legalization process: Make sure it is ready and compliant with upcoming international cryptocurrency regulations. This ensures the preservation of your work and prevents unexpected events from undermining your efforts to establish a new cryptocurrency.

6.3.4 Cryptocurrency mining reward

The primary focus of cryptocurrency mining rewards is the discussion of the impact of the spilling event on the profitability of miners and the incentives to proceed with mining. Examine the impact of transaction fees on the overall functionality of the cryptocurrency network. Analyze the potential future implications for the cryptocurrency market if transaction fees become the primary revenue source for miners and consider the potential impact of declining block rewards on miner behavior and network security over time. Cryptocurrency mining rewards are the sum of money that miners earn for validating and adding new transactions to a blockchain. The reward usually comes in two forms:

Block Reward: Miners receive newly created the digital currency when they solve the cryptographic challenge and add a new block to the blockchain.

Transaction Fees: In addition to the block reward, miners receive transaction fees from users for include their transactions in the block. These costs can vary depending on network demand and the number of transactions waiting to be completed.

6.3.5 Pricing Cryptocurrencies

To understand cryptocurrency pricing, let's take the most famous example of Bitcoin. The interaction of supply and demand as well as expectations for future prices determines the price of Bitcoin, just like it does for most other commodities in the market. For cryptocurrencies, pricing is entirely based on market dynamics. If the market believes that the price of Bitcoin will rise in the future, they will now be more people who are ready to pay more for it. In contrast, if the market expects the price to fall, more people will sell cryptocurrencies now, raising the price. When selling, there are many people who accept lower prices than usual and expect lower prices in the future. Many individual influencers can also significantly influence the price of cryptocurrencies.

Forbes listed the top five cryptocurrencies in the market in 2022 as follows:

- The market capitalization of Bitcoin (BTC) is $880 billion.

- The market capitalization of Ethereum (ETH) is $415 billion.

- Tether (USDT): The market capitalization of Tether (USDT) exceeds $79 billion.

- Binance Coin (BNB): The market capitalization of Binance Coin (BNB) exceeds $68 billion.

- S. Dollar Coin (USDC): The USDC has a market capitalization of more than $53 billion.

Cryptocurrencies such as Bitcoin and Ethereum are essentially the result of a protocol or program that employs a certain technology or platform. When we say "investing in cryptocurrency," it means investing in the protocol. You can convert the cryptocurrency product to a real-world currency for future usage. In cryptocurrency, "miners" create or generate "coins" (publicly agreed records of ownership). These miners execute programs on ASIC (application-specific integrated circuit) devices designed specifically for proof-of-work puzzles. The work required to mine coins gives them worth, while coin scarcity and demand allow their value to fluctuate.

6.4 Coins and Tokens

Cryptocurrencies are classified into two categories: coins and tokens. A coin is a cryptocurrency program that operates on its own blockchain, facilitating all transactions therein. Tokens operate on established blockchain technology and are generally utilized for tangible items like as smart contracts and digital services.

Blockchain technology creates cryptocurrencies and tokens. Please note that blockchain systems do not include crypto tokens directly. The apps are built on current technology and typically use smart contracts for various functionalities. Coins represent traditional currency, whereas tokens represent assets or deeds. A crypto token might represent a DAO share, digital product, NFT, or real thing. Crypto tokens may be bought, sold, and exchanged like coins. However, they are rarely used for trade. Crypto tokens are like coupons or vouchers, whereas crypto coins are like dollars and cents.

Cryptocurrencies are divided into two groups: coins and tokens. Coins are applications running on their own blockchain, while tokens work on existing blockchain infrastructure and are used for physical objects like smart contracts. Coins represent traditional currency, while tokens represent assets or deeds, and can be bought, sold, and exchanged like coins.

6.4.1 Create Coin and Token

a) Creating a coin: Creating a cryptocurrency (coin) on a blockchain involves several steps, from defining the parameters of the coin to deploying it on a blockchain network. While this process can vary depending on the blockchain platform you choose (e.g., Ethereum, Binance Smart Chain, or even creating a custom blockchain), here is a general step-by-step guide to creating your own coin:

Step 1: Purpose of the coin.

Step 2: Platform Selection

Step 3: Generate coin

Step 4: Validate the coin

Step 5: Publish with Smart Contrac

b) Creating a Token: The token is compatible with the current blockchain architecture, as was already mentioned. Therefore, if you create your token on a high-performance blockchain like Ethereum, it should function on a highly secure network and safeguard against fraud assaults. When you use a consensus method and leverage your current decentralized infrastructure, tokenization is less expensive both in terms of money and time.

6.5 Bitcoin

In this world, a variety of currencies are used for trading amenities. The rupee, dollar, pound, euro, and yen are some of the currencies that are commonly used for trading. These are printed currencies and coins, some of which you may already have in your wallet. But bitcoin is a currency you cannot touch, you cannot see, but you can efficiently use to trade amenities. It is an electronically stored currency. You can store it as a virtual currency on your mobiles, computers, or any other storage media. Bitcoin is an innovative and digital payment system. It is an example of a cryptocurrency and the next big thing in finance.

Physically, a normal piece of paper and a currency note are identical, but an authority or a centralized government determines the note's value. But Bitcoin is a currency that does not have any centralized government or authority to control and decide its value. It is a decentralized digital currency. As of now (October 2024), the value of 1 bitcoin is 114350.58 Indian rupees, but this value fluctuates as there is no centralized authority to control. In December 2011, experts estimated the value of bitcoin to be 2 US dollars, and in December 2013, it surged to approximately 1000 US dollars.

6.5.1 Bitcoin Mining

The process involves verifying bitcoin transactions and storing them in a blockchain, also known as a ledger. The miner is the person who solves mathematical puzzles (also called proof of work) to validate the transaction. Anyone with mining hardware and computing power can participate in this. Numerous miners participate simultaneously to solve the complex mathematical puzzle; the one who solves it first wins 12.5 bitcoin as a part of the reward. After solving the puzzle, the miner verifies the transactions and then adds the confirmed block to the blockchain. The blockchain contains the history of every transaction that has taken place in the network. Once the minor adds the block to the blockchain, bitcoins are then transferred, which were associated with the transaction.

For the miners to earn rewards from verifying the bitcoin transactions, two things must be ensured:

1. The miners must verify the one-megabyte size of the transaction.

2. For the addition of a new block of transactions in the blockchain, miners must have the ability to solve complex computational math problems called proof for work by finding a 64-bit hexadecimal hash value.

Bitcoin operates as a decentralized digital currency, enabling peer-to-peer transfers regardless of geographical location without the need for an intermediary such as a bank or administrator. Satoshi Nakamoto first created it in 2009. Compared to traditional currency, Bitcoin offers the following advantages:

i)   Bitcoin offers lower transaction fees than traditional online payment mechanisms.

ii) The government issues normal currencies, but bitcoin operates in a decentralized manner.

iii) There is no tax in bitcoin, unlike normal currency, where one has to pay tax.

iv) No third-party seizure occurs in bitcoin, as there's no central authority responsible for this.

v)   No one can track the bitcoin except the owner and receiver of it.

It is a cryptocurrency, and the transactions related to bitcoins take place in the blockchain network. A virtual wallet stores each bitcoin, and a transaction involves transferring it from one wallet to another. Peers can send bitcoins without any intermediary, such as a bank, regardless of their geographical location. It works in a decentralized way, meaning nobody can interfere with your digital money; only you are responsible for your bitcoins.

6.5.2 How Bitcoin Transactions Work

We digitally sign Bitcoin transactions for security. Everyone on the network gets to know about a transaction. A transaction contains 3 pieces of information. The sender's bitcoin wallet address appears in the first part, followed by the sent amount in the second, and the recipient's bitcoin wallet address in the third. A bitcoin can also be considered an invisible currency with only the transaction records between different addresses. A public ledger known as a blockchain stores every transaction ever made using Bitcoin.

There are four basic components of bitcoin:

1. Software: Bitcoin is, at its heart, a piece of software that defines what bitcoin is and how it is transmitted. In addition to verifying bitcoin's legitimacy, it controls its use. The type of regulation of a legitimate bitcoin is established via it. Software, specifically the bitcoin program, powers everything. The bitcoin program is always available 24 hours a day, seven days a week (24X7).

2. Cryptography: The software revolves around cryptography and bitcoin as a cryptocurrency. Bitcoin regulates both the transfer of bitcoins between parties and the production of new bitcoin units using encryption. Without cryptography, Bitcoin would not exist. We have established that this software utilizes cryptography to regulate bitcoin transfers across the internet. Only machines, not people, can solve the mathematical approach known as cryptography. Cryptography is required to safeguard the data.

3. Hardware: To run and solve cryptography, a significant amount of hardware is required. The creators specifically designed this gear for mining, which involves detecting Nonce to validate blocks and hashes. Simple activities on the bitcoin blockchain require a significant amount of CPU power. If one tries to mine bitcoin with a smartphone or home computer right now, you'll lose your computer and rack up a large electric bill.

4. Miners (Gaming Theory): Game theory studies rational decision-making behavior in humans. Game theory allows interactions between two or more players in a system where the participant's outcome is based on the actions of the others. Every participant's aim is to maximize his gain. Bitcoin uses the game theory to ensure that rational individuals align their interests in a specific way. These factors significantly

influence the interactions and behavior of miners within the network. Miners are individuals who participate in a gaming theory, as bitcoin is essentially a game that is played by miners all over the world. The first component, as mentioned above, is bitcoin software that issues a cryptography challenge every 10 minutes. The cryptography task entails locating a nonce that will allow the hash of a certain block to be legitimate.

6.5 Various Cryptocurrencies

Thousands of cryptocurrencies serve distinct functions and use cases. Here are some of the most famous cryptocurrencies:

6.5.1 Litecoin

A disagreement on the Bitcoin blockchain led to the creation of Litecoin (LTC), a cryptocurrency. Litecoin developed to address concerns about Bitcoin's increasing centralization and to hinder the power of large-scale mining operations over the mining process. Despite the fact that Litecoin's efforts to prevent enterprise-level miners from controlling the network ultimately failed, the cryptocurrency has developed into a peer-to-peer payment system and a coin that is broadly minable. One of its primary objectives was to employ an alternative encryption method to restrict the influence of large miners. However, industrial miners were able to expand their capacity as a result of the rapid adaptation of specialized machinery.

Similar to Bitcoin, Litecoin can be mined using ASIC miners. A block on a blockchain contains transaction information. The block is validated by mining software and made available to any system participant (referred to as a miner) who wants to examine it. When a miner validates it, the next block in the chain is generated, and Litecoin is awarded.

Litecoin (LTC) is a cryptocurrency launched in 2011 as a fork of Bitcoin, aimed at decentralizing mining and enhancing peer-to-peer payments. Despite its initial goal to limit large-scale mining control, it has become minable like Bitcoin using ASIC miners, with transaction data stored in blocks verified by miners.

Scrypt (pronounced "es-crypt") is the hashing algorithm used by Litecoin. Scrypt requires larger amounts of memory and runs slower than

SHA-256. However, it gained acceptance in the cryptocurrency world after the 2011 Tenebrix project updated Scrypt to run with standard CPUs for mining. Scrypt's high memory needs hampered the development of ASIC miners. However, the ASIC-resistant arrangement was short-lived, with the world witnessing the release of the first Litecoin ASIC miner in 2016.

Litecoin can be sold on the same exchanges where it is purchased; however, the process varies between centralized and decentralized exchanges. For example, when selling Litecoin on a centralized exchange such as Kraken, you must first transfer your LTC to your Kraken wallet address. The exchange will subsequently manage the sale for you. On decentralized exchanges such as KuCoin or Crypto.com, you will link your wallet directly to the platform. Prior to initiating trading, it is typically necessary to undergo a "Know Your Customer (KYC)" verification process. After receiving approval, you may proceed to deposit your Litecoin and sell it. Certain exchanges permit the withdrawal of fiat currency, so if you're looking to convert your LTC to cash, ensure that the exchange accommodates fiat withdrawals.

Some common use cases of Litecoin are:

a) Peer-to-Peer Payments: Litecoin serves as digital currency for daily transactions, providing quicker and more affordable transfers than Bitcoin.

b) Merchant Adoption: Many online and offline merchants accept Litecoin due to its fast transaction times and low fees.

c) Testing Ground for Bitcoin Features: As a complementary network, Litecoin frequently acts as a testing ground for features like SegWit that Bitcoin might eventually implement.

6.5.2 Ethereum

Ethereum is a blockchain network that introduced a built-in, Turing-complete programming language, enabling the creation of decentralized applications (DApps). Its native cryptocurrency, ether (ETH), powers the network. Ethereum is renowned for its ability to support smart contracts, which are self-executing contracts that incorporate the agreement's terms directly into the code. Imagine these as "cryptographic bank lockers" that store value and unlock only upon the fulfilment of predetermined conditions. Solidity, an object-oriented programming language that is relatively easy to learn, serves as the primary language for writing smart contracts. The EVM is the runtime environment that processes smart contracts and DApps on the Ethereum blockchain. It ensures that decentralized applications run smoothly across all nodes in the network, maintaining consistency and security.

While Bitcoin is designed mainly as a payment network focusing on the financial sector, Ethereum's versatility allows it to be applied across various industries, making it a platform for more than just financial transactions. Ethereum's broader scope has earned it the moniker "Blockchain 2.0," demonstrating the potential of blockchain technology beyond the realm of finance.

Ethereum currently uses a Proof of Stake (PoS) consensus mechanism, which is more energy-efficient compared to Bitcoin's Proof of Work (PoW). In PoS, the ability to validate transactions and create new blocks depends on the amount of cryptocurrency (stake) a node holds, reducing the energy-intensive computation required in PoW.

Ethereum has two types of accounts: externally owned accounts (EOA) and contract accounts. These are explained as follows below.

Private keys control externally owned accounts (EOAs). Each EOA has a public-private key pair. The users can send messages by creating and signing transactions.

Contract codes govern contract accounts. The account stores these codes. Each contract account has an ether balance associated with it. Every time these accounts receive a transaction from an EOA or a message from another contract, they activate their contract code. When the contract code activates, it allows to read/write the message to the local storage, send messages, and create contracts.

> *Ethereum is a blockchain network that enables the creation of decentralized applications (Dapps) using a Turing-complete programming language. It operates on its cryptocurrency, ether, and is known for its smart contracts, which function like conditional cryptographic lockers. Smart contracts are primarily developed in Solidity, an easy-to-learn programming language. Unlike Bitcoin, which focuses solely on financial transactions, Ethereum supports various applications across different sectors, earning it the nickname Blockchain 2.0. It uses a Proof of Stake (PoS) consensus mechanism, which is more energy-efficient than Bitcoin's Proof of Work (PoW).*

In 2022, Ethereum transitioned from its original Proof of Work (PoW) consensus mechanism to Proof of Stake (PoS) in a major upgrade known as "The Merge." This shift aimed to improve scalability, security, and energy efficiency. Instead of using energy-intensive mining, PoS selects validators to create new blocks and validate transactions based on the amount of ether they hold and "stake" in the network.

Here are some common use cases of Ethereum:

a) Decentralized Finance (DeFi): Ethereum is the backbone of DeFi, enabling users to access financial services like lending, borrowing, and trading without intermediaries.

b) Non-Fungible Tokens (NFTs): Ethereum is the leading platform for NFTs, which represent unique digital assets such as art, music, and virtual property.

c) Supply Chain Management: Ethereum's transparency and immutability make it ideal for tracking goods and verifying authenticity in supply chains.

d) Gaming and Virtual Worlds: Ethereum supports blockchain-based games and virtual worlds, where players can own, trade, and monetize in-game assets.

e) Ethereum continues to evolve, with ongoing upgrades aimed at enhancing network performance and reducing transaction fees, ensuring it stays at the forefront of the blockchain ecosystem.

6.5.3 Altcoin

Altcoins (short for "alternative coins") are generally defined as all cryptocurrencies other than Bitcoin (BTC). However, because most cryptocurrencies fork from either Bitcoin or Ethereum (ETH), some people consider altcoins to be all cryptocurrencies other than these two. Some popular altcoins are Ethereum (ETH), Binance Coin (BNB), Ripple (XRP), Litecoin (LTC), and Cardano (ADA). Different altcoins use different consensus mechanisms to validate transactions and open new blocks, or they attempt to distinguish themselves from Bitcoin and Ethereum by providing new or additional capabilities or purposes. Developers design and release most altcoins, each with a unique vision or purpose for their tokens or cryptocurrency. Learn more about altcoins and what makes them different from Bitcoin. "Altcoin" is a combination of the two words "alternative" and "coin." Generally, it encompasses all cryptocurrencies and tokens that do not belong to Bitcoin. Altcoins belong to the blockchains they were explicitly designed for. Many are forks, a splitting of a blockchain that is not compatible with the original chain from Bitcoin and Ethereum. These forks generally have more than one reason for occurring. Most of the time, a group of developers disagrees with others and decides to create their own coin.

The primary distinction between altcoins and bitcoin lies in their technological differences: Many altcoins offer technological advancements or different consensus mechanisms compared to Bitcoin. The second is **purpose:** While Bitcoin originated as a decentralized digital currency, numerous altcoins aim to enhance privacy, facilitate decentralized finance (DeFi), or bolster DApps, and third is **Consensus Mechanisms:** While Bitcoin uses Proof of Work (PoW), many altcoins, such as Cardano and Ethereum (since Ethereum 2.0), use Proof of Stake (PoS) or other mechanisms that are considered more energy efficient.

Altcoins are cryptocurrencies and tokens that are not Bitcoin (BTC), but some consider them crytocurrencies other than Bitcoin and Ethereum (ETH). They are designed by developers with different visions or uses for their tokens or cryptocurrency. Altcoins aim to improve upon the limitations of the original blockchains they are forked from or competing with. The first altcoin was Litecoin, forked from Bitcoin in 2011, using a different proof-of-work (PoW) mechanism called Scrypt. Ether, designed to support Ethereum, is used to pay network participants for transaction validation work.

6.6 Wallet

Wallets are just like your Account number, but the difference is that it lets you store the cryptocurrency. It can support single or multiple cryptocurrencies.

- It allows the instant transaction, which saves the time

- Record the history of the transaction

- Solve the problem of maintaining various blockchain accounts and balances.

- It can be single signed or multiple signed wallets.

6.6.1 Procedure To Create a Wallet

1. We can create our own wallet by signing up in mobile apps, or web apps, for desktop wallets you need to install the application for it.

2. Once you sign up in mobile apps or web apps you are provided with the public key and private key. The public key is your wallet address and the private key will indicate that you are the owner of this account.

3. A seed phrase (also called a recovery phrase) is generated as a backup to restore access to your wallet if lost. Write it down and store it securely offline. Never share it with anyone.

4. Remember you can create as many wallets as you can, but your account will only be visible in the network when you will perform any transaction.

6.6.2 Wallet Types

In this section, we will be discussing the types of wallets on the basis of their functionality. These are:

1. **Hot wallet:** These wallets are connected to the internet which made them more accessible to the user. They are easier to set up but they are more prone to hackers and technical vulnerabilities. *Examples:* Coinbase, Metamask

2. **Cold wallet:** These wallets are not connected to the internet, they are more secure than hot wallets. *Examples:* Trezor, Ledger Nano

3. **Software wallet:** It can be a web wallet, desktop wallet, or mobile wallet.

a) **Web** wallets: Web wallets are hot wallets that are always connected to the internet and can be accessed through different browsers such as Google Chrome, Firefox, and Internet Explorer. *Example:* Metamask, MyEther Wallet.

b) **Desktop Wallet:** Desktop wallets are installable software packs that are available for most of the desktop operating systems such as Mac, Windows, Linux.

Examples Electrum, Exodus

c) **Mobile wallet:** Mobile wallets are the fourth most secure way to store your cryptocurrencies because they are always connected to the internet (hot wallets) and can be flawed by its development community itself.it is available on both IOS and Android.

Examples– Coinbase, Coinomi

4. **Hardware wallet:** These wallets are physical, electronic devices that use a random number generator to generate public keys. The keys are stored in the device itself which is not connected to the internet. Hardware devices built specifically for handling private keys and public addresses. *Examples*– Ledger Nano S, Keepkey

5. **Physical/Paper wallet:** It is a piece of paper in which address and private keys are physically printed. Needless to say, as it keeps your private keys offline, it is another secure way of storing your cryptos but not all cryptocurrencies offer paper wallets. *Examples*- Ethereum paper wallet.

6.6.3 Advantages of Cryptocurrency Wallet

i)   Decentralized: It means there is no central authority to control the network.

ii) Transparency: Since every transaction is stored on the blockchain, in case of any discrepancy we can check the record.

iii) International use: You can do Inter-Country transactions very easily because there are no banks involved between this.

iv) Low operation cost: When you transfer money from one bank account to another, they charge a considerable amount of money to complete the transaction. If you transfer cryptocurrency, it will charge very little amount.

v) Instant transfer: Cryptocurrency is transferred instantly which makes the transaction fast and saves time, irrespective of the geographical location of the sender and receiver.

6.6.4 Disadvantages of Cryptocurrency Wallet

i) Universal Acceptance: Cryptocurrency is not accepted worldwide, in some countries, it's not legal tender.

ii) Price fluctuation: The price of cryptocurrency fluctuates very much, as you can see the price of bitcoin on March, 20 was $6483.74 and on May, 20 it was $9, 437.05.

iii) Keeping the seed phrase secret: If you don't keep phrase secure, the security of your account can be compromised

iv) Reversing the payment: If you mistakenly pay someone by using cryptocurrency, then there is no way to get a refund of the amount paid. All you can do is to ask the person for a refund and if your request is turned down, then just forget about the money.

6.7 Cryptocurrency Fraud and Cryptocurrency Scams

Unfortunately, there has been a rise in criminal activities associated with cryptocurrency. It is important for individuals to be aware of the different types of cryptocurrency scams.

Fake websites: There are numerous fraudulent websites that display fabricated testimonials and use complex cryptocurrency terminology to make unrealistic promises of substantial and guaranteed returns, as long as you continue to invest.

Virtual Ponzi schemes: Criminals engaged in the cryptocurrency sector perpetrate misleading activities through the promotion of suspicious investment prospects in digital currencies. They deceive individuals by employing funds from new investors to compensate earlier investors, thereby creating the false impression of substantial returns.

"Celebrity" endorsements: Scammers conduct online transactions under fake identities of millionaires or celebrities in order to solicit funds to augment virtual currency investments. Instead of fulfilling their promises, these crooks take the money. People may even use messaging applications or chat forums to spread allegations that a famous businessperson endorses a cryptocurrency. Scammers trick investors into buying, raising prices. After doing this, they sell their shares, lowering the currency's value.

Scammers might set up fake exchanges or seem like actual virtual currency shops to steal money. Another crypto scam involves false sales presentations for cryptocurrency-denominated retirement funds. There's also direct cryptocurrency hacking, where attackers steal consumers' virtual cash from digital purses.

Test your skill

1. What do you understand by Cryptocurrency?

2. What is digital currency?

3. Write the Difference between digital currency and cryptocurrency.

4. Discus the various Cryptocurrency fraud and cryptocurrency scams.

5. What is Wallet? Discuss the various type of Wallet

6. Write the Difference between hardware and software wallet.

7. Write the advantage and disadvantage of cryptocurrency wallet.

8. What do you understand by Bitcoin Mining?

9. Explain the bitcoin mining process.

10. discus the various Components of Bitcoin

11. What is Ethereum?

12. What is Ether.

13. What is alternat coin.

14. What is the need of alternat coin?

15. explain the Markle tree hash.

16. Discus the difference between coin and token.

17. discuss the various Platform for Generating Cryptocurrency.

18. How does cryptocurrency work?

Chapter – 7

INTEGRATION OF BLOCKCHAIN TECHNOLOGY WITH OTHER CUTTING-EDGE TECHNOLOGIES

The integration of blockchain technology with other technologies has the potential to revolutionize various industries by creating innovative and powerful solutions. Integrating blockchain technology can create valuable synergies and open up new possibilities across various industries. This chapter will delve deeper into the various ways to seamlessly integrate blockchain with other cutting-edge technologies.

7.1 Integrated Blockchain Technology with Cloud Computing

Cloud computing is the convenient and flexible way to access computing services, including servers, storage, databases, networking, software, and analytics. Instead of storing files on a private internal drive or local storage device, cloud-based storage allows for remote saving. Cloud computing has enormous potential, but consumer adoption has lagged. Consumers are hesitant to use cloud computing, especially cloud storage, due to data security concerns and other potential hazards. In addition to its unique structures, cloud computing inherits classic security and privacy problems. Cloud computing has some drawbacks. The provider may fail to detect employee insider attacks. Consumer-provider agreements may be opaque. Other concerns include data loss, traffic hijacking, and common technology and application interface vulnerabilities. Figure 7.1 mentions the major pros and cons.

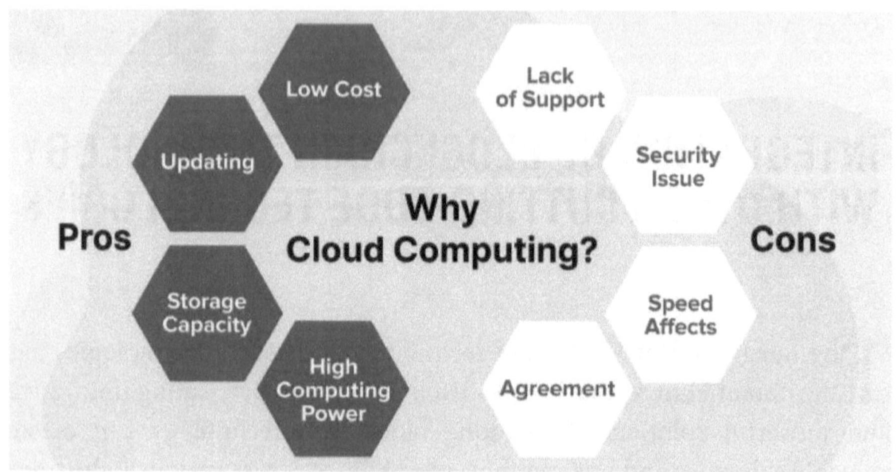

Figure 7.1: Strength and scope of cloud computing.

Cloud computing and blockchain are revolutionary technologies with the ability to transform industries and give a high level of trust and security for sensitive data while retaining anonymity. To investigate the integration of cloud computing and blockchain, it is required to examine their various characteristics, as described in Table 7.1.

Cloud Computing	Blockchain Technology
Cloud computing is an internet-based hosting service in which organizations provide storage capacity and processing resources via the internet.	*Blockchain is an impressive, decentralized ledger that guarantees the security and integrity of data records, preventing any tampering or alteration.*
Cloud computing allows you to conveniently store all of your information in one central location but maintain the location transparency with other users.	*Blockchain technology enables the decentralized storage of data across various global locations, ensuring that each node maintains a copy of the information.*
In contrast to blockchain's peer-to-peer design, cloud computing relies heavily on the involvement of multiple intermediary companies.	*Blockchain functions autonomously, eliminating the necessity for third-party service providers and granting individuals full control over its network.*
It provides increased flexibility, allowing you to access your files from various devices.	*Blockchain is restricted to certain protocols.*
Data is mutable	*Data is immutable*

Similar to cloud computing, blockchain technology offers numerous benefits for processing transactions and data.

Blockchain can facilitate decentralized cloud storage solutions by distributing data across a network of nodes, thereby enhancing security and decreasing dependence on individual providers. These solutions can automate cloud service agreements and transactions, ensuring transparent and automatic execution of terms between parties. It is capable of tracking and managing data access and transactions across various cloud environments.

The integration of cloud computing and blockchain technology effectively addresses the fundamental issues of security and privacy. The decentralized and distributed nature of blockchain technology also contributes to enhancing transparency. Integrating blockchain technology with cloud computing has numerous benefits. Here are some of them:

a. **Security:** The decentralized nature of blockchain and the use of cryptographic algorithms guarantee the integrity of data. Consensus from multiple nodes is necessary for any changes to the data, which adds a layer of security and makes unauthorized alterations quite challenging. Cloud-based blockchain systems have the ability to significantly improve the security of transactions and communications. Blockchain's powerful encryption and decentralized verification mechanisms achieve this.

b. **Transparency and Accountability:** The blockchain technology offers an immutable ledger of transactions, making it highly valuable for auditing and monitoring alterations in cloud environments. The execution of predefined actions by automated smart contracts based on specific conditions helps minimize the need for manual intervention and enhances accountability.

c. **Decentralization:** Blockchain has the potential to decrease dependence on a single point of control or failure. In cloud environments, there is a reduced likelihood of central server breaches or outages that could impact the entire system. Blockchain technology enables the achievement of distributed cloud storage solutions. This allows for the fragmentation and storage of data across multiple nodes, thereby enhancing data redundancy and availability.

d. **Data Ownership and Privacy:** Data owners can maintain authority over their data and authorize access privileges through identity management systems based on blockchain technology. Blockchain technology enables the implementation of privacy-preserving methods, such as zero-knowledge proofs, thereby improving data privacy in cloud environments.

The integration of blockchain with cloud computing can greatly improve security, transparency, and efficiency, while also opening up new opportunities for decentralized applications and services. It is essential to carefully consider scalability, complexity, and regulatory factors in order to effectively leverage these technologies in conjunction with each other.

7.2 Blockchain Technology in Artificial Intelligence

Artificial intelligence and blockchain are widely acknowledged by IT companies as significantly disruptive technologies. Individually, they have the potential to completely transform a wide range of industries, as well as the economic and social landscape. The integration of AI and blockchain technology opens up a world of possibilities, enabling a new generation of applications that leverage the increased productivity and enhanced security and transparency. The capabilities of deep learning models are truly impressive. Their capacity to handle vast quantities of data, identify patterns, make precise predictions, and support decision-making is truly impressive. They achieve this by employing intricate neural networks that closely resemble the cognitive processes of the human brain. The blockchain network provides a transparent, decentralized, and resilient economic settlement layer on the internet. It allows for secure data storage and digital interactions independently of trust or permission.

This powerful integration of blockchain and AI allows automated decision-making systems to produce precise and reliable findings with real-world implications. The most reliable data is immutable and tamper-proof.

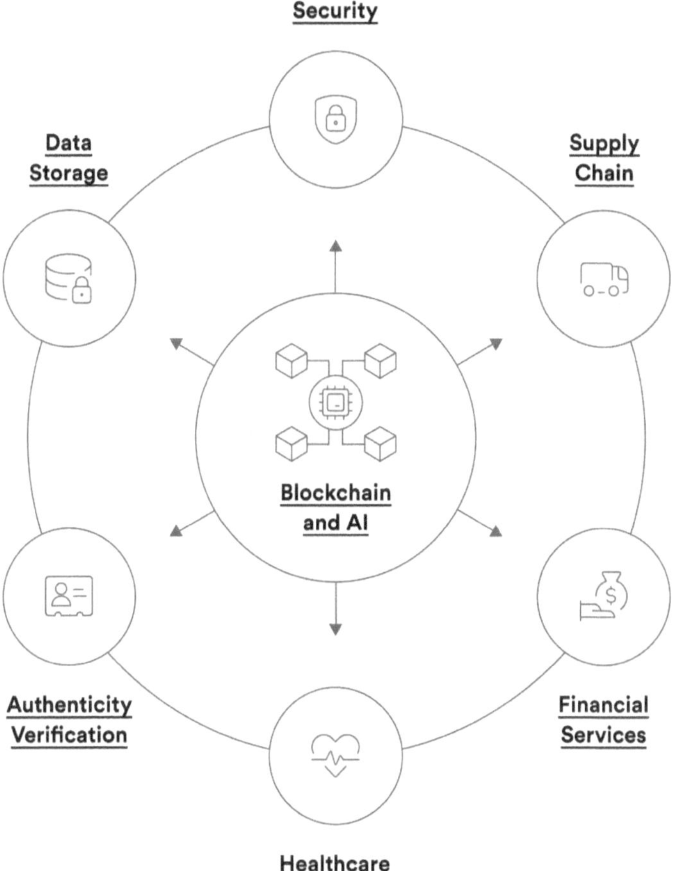

Figure 7.2: Integration of Blockchain Technology and Artificial Intelligence

The integration of blockchain and AI holds the promise to transform business models, enhance operational efficiency for companies, automate routine tasks for individuals, facilitate secure and effective data sharing, elevate decision-making with AI-powered smart contracts, and promote trust and transparency in essential infrastructure and economic systems. This section will delve into various potential use cases that demonstrate the influence of AI and blockchain integrations.

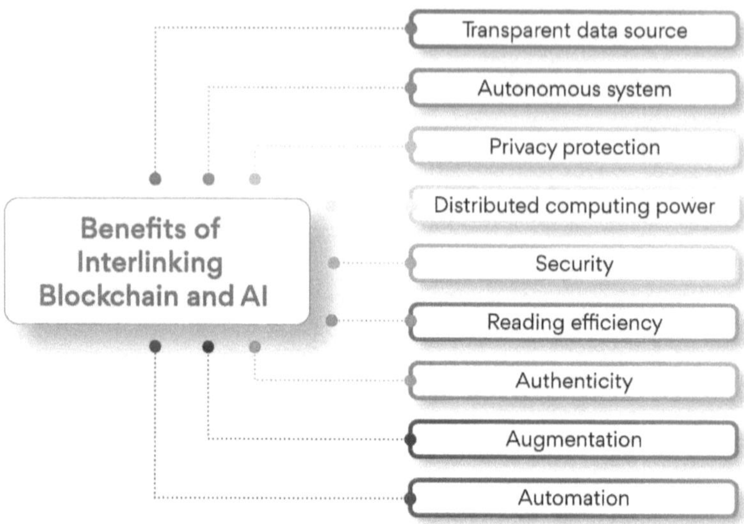

Figure 7.3 interlinked of AI with Blockchain Technology

7.2.1 Combined values of blockchain and AI

a) Authenticity: The blockchain's digital record offers transparency regarding the framework that underpins AI and the source of the data it employs, addressing the challenge of explainable AI. This comprehension boosts trust in the reliability of data and the recommendations provided by AI. Utilizing blockchain for the storage and distribution of AI models establishes a dependable audit trail, and the integration of blockchain with AI can greatly enhance data security.

b) Augmentation: AI has the capacity to read, comprehend, and correlate data at remarkable speeds, thereby introducing a new level of intelligence to blockchain-based business networks rapidly and comprehensively. Blockchain enables AI to scale effectively by providing access to a vast amount of data from both internal and external sources. This results in the development of a transparent and dependable data economy, enhanced management of data utilization and model sharing, and the acquisition of more actionable insights.

c) Automation: AI, automation, and blockchain have the potential to improve business processes that involve multiple stakeholders by reducing friction, increasing speed, and increasing efficiency. AI models, when incorporated into smart contracts operating on a blockchain, can perform the following actions:

i) suggest that expired products be recalled.

ii) Execute transactions, including re-orders, payments, and stock purchases, in accordance with established thresholds and events.

iii) Resolve disputes.

iv) Determine the most environmentally friendly transportation method.

7.2.2 Use cases for blockchain and AI

Across industries, bringing AI into blockchain delivers new opportunities

a) Healthcare

Artificial intelligence can enhance nearly every domain in healthcare, from uncovering therapeutic ideas and addressing user requirements to analyzing patient data and recognizing patterns. Utilizing blockchain for patient data, including electronic health records, enables companies to collaborate to improve care while safeguarding patient privacy.

b) Life sciences

Blockchain and artificial intelligence in the pharmaceutical sector can enhance visibility and traceability inside the drug supply chain while significantly improving the success rate of clinical trials. The integration of modern data analysis with a decentralized architecture for clinical trials ensures data integrity, transparency, patient tracking, permission management, and the automation of trial participation and data gathering.

c) Financial services

Blockchain and artificial intelligence are revolutionizing the financial services sector by fostering trust, eliminating friction in multiparty transactions, and enhancing transaction speed. Examine the loan procedure. Applicants authorize access to personal records maintained on the blockchain. Reliance on data and automated evaluation processes for applications facilitates expedited closings and enhances client satisfaction.

d)   Supply chain

Blockchain and artificial intelligence (AI) are revolutionizing supply chains across industries and opening up new opportunities by digitizing a process that was previously primarily paper-based, making data trustworthy and shareable, and adding intelligence and automation to perform transactions. To improve decarbonization efforts, for instance, a company can collect carbon emissions data at the product or parts level.

e)   Banking and Related Services

Blockchain technology and artificial intelligence have the potential to change the financial services industry by enhancing efficiency, security, and transparency to a greater extent. The immutability and integrity of financial data are both guaranteed by blockchain technology, and algorithms powered by artificial intelligence are able to detect fraudulent conduct in blockchain transactions.

7.2.3 Problems and Issues to Consider with AI in Blockchain

The use of artificial intelligence (AI) in blockchain technology, or "AI in blockchain," offers both potential and particular difficulties. Let's examine a few of the most important factors in this creative combination.

a)   Security and Privacy of Data

Blockchain requires data privacy to be maintained, and adding AI complicates matters further. For training, AI algorithms require access to data, yet protecting the privacy and security of sensitive data can be difficult. It becomes essential to have strong encryption and access control systems in place.

b)   The Ability to Scale

Blockchain and artificial intelligence require a lot of resources. Scalability becomes a major challenge when coupled. Potential bottlenecks may result from the computing needs of AI algorithms and the expanding scale of blockchain networks. It's crucial to provide effective scaling solutions for seamless integration.

c)   Interoperability

To fully realize the promise of AI and blockchain, compatibility between the two platforms must be ensured. Blockchain protocols and various AI models cannot always exchange or easily transmit data. Smoother integration may be achieved by bridging this gap through the standardization of interfaces and protocols.

d)   Algorithmic Bias

Biases included in the data used to train AI systems can affect them. These biases can provide unfair or biased results when combined with blockchain, weakening the system's openness and reliability. To properly address algorithmic biases, careful thought and mitigation techniques are required.

e)   Regulatory Compliance

Blockchain technology and artificial intelligence present complicated regulatory issues. It becomes critical to abide by banking rules, data protection laws, and other legal frameworks. It takes careful balance to create AI-driven blockchain solutions that respect legal standards without sacrificing innovation.

f)   Security of Smart Contracts

Smart contracts are essential parts of blockchain systems that automate the performance of pre-arranged contracts. Artificial intelligence (AI) adds additional security threats to smart contracts, such as manipulation of transactions led by AI or weaknesses in AI decision-making processes. To reduce these risks, extensive testing and auditing are necessary.

7.2.4 A Futuristic Approach

When artificial intelligence and blockchain are combined, they can help you build an immutable, safe, and decentralized system. This method will lead to major data and information security advances in different industries.

But, the convergence of artificial intelligence and blockchain technology is still unexplored. Even though the integration of the two technologies has attracted considerable attention. Also, projects are devoted to the ground-breaking combination that is available. Bringing the two technologies together will enable data to be used under unimaginable circumstances.

With each of these technologies affecting and executing data in different ways, their collaboration will make a logical explanation. It has the potential to push data exploitation to newer heights.

7.3 Blockchain Technology with Internet of Things

In the rapidly expanding world of the Internet of Things (IoT), where everyday objects are interconnected and communicate vast amounts of data, the security of these networks is paramount. Blockchain technology, known for underpinning cryptocurrencies like Bitcoin, offers a promising solution to secure IoT networks, ensuring data integrity and privacy for connected devices. The integration of the Internet of Things (IoT) with blockchain technology marks a pivotal evolution in how devices interact, enhancing security, trust, and efficiency across numerous industries.

The IoT ecosystem, a network of interconnected devices, brings convenience and automation to daily life and operations across industries. By embedding sensors and actuaries in physical objects, IoT transforms them into smart, responsive tools that communicate over the internet. However, as the number of connected devices grows, so does the complexity of managing them and the data they generate, highlighting the need for enhanced security and scalable solutions.

The Internet of Things (IoT) and blockchain technology are transforming the way we communicate and interact, opening up numerous examples of how connected devices can benefit from the decentralized approach, transparency and traceability, reliability, tamper-proof characteristics, and automation offered by blockchain. IoT with blockchain refers to the use of a cryptographically secure digital ledger to authenticate, store, and share data generated by connected devices, in a reliable way that prevents that data from being falsified, corrupted, or altered. Examples of IoT and blockchain technology working together span many different industries and domains, including security, healthcare, the supply chain, and the Industrial Internet of Things (IIoT).

7.3.1 The Promise of Blockchain in IoT

Blockchain technology offers a decentralized and secure framework for IoT, addressing core challenges such as cyber security, scalability, and trust. Through cryptography and a distributed ledger, blockchain ensures the integrity and verifiability of data across the IoT network, making it resistant to tampering and cyber-attacks.

a)   Enhancing Security and Trust

One of the primary benefits of integrating blockchain with IoT is the significant enhancement of security. By enabling tamper-proof and secure communication between devices, blockchain mitigates risks associated with cyber threats and data breaches, ensuring that connected devices are less vulnerable to attacks.

b)   Decentralization and Efficiency

Blockchain's decentralized nature eliminates the need for a central authority, reducing potential bottlenecks and vulnerabilities. This decentralization not only enhances the security of IoT networks but also improves their scalability and efficiency, facilitating smoother operations and maintenance.

c)   Authentication

With billions of data points logged from thousands or even millions of IIoT sensors, blockchain introduces much-needed authentication for data, ensuring it is secure and tamper-proof on a decentralized ledger of data transactions. As such, blockchain helps IIoT use cases meet their compliance, auditing, and regulatory requirements

7.3.2 Challenges of IoT and Blockchain

a)   Scalability

IoT generates massive amounts of data, which can pose a challenge for blockchain networks in terms of throughput and latency.

b) Compute and Storage

IoT devices are typically designed to be small, low-cost, and low-power, with their main purpose being to gather and transmit data. As a result, IoT devices often have limited compute and storage capabilities, meaning they may struggle to run demanding blockchain software applications and process/store large amounts of data. Problematically, blockchain needs significant computing power to perform the complex mathematical calculations required to validate transactions, as well as storage, because each node in the network must maintain a copy of the entire blockchain.

c) Interoperability

IoT devices may use different protocols and standards (e.g., MQTT and HTTP), making it difficult to integrate them into a common blockchain network. Presently, there are only a small number of standards available for the integration of IoT and blockchain, leading to reduced interoperability.

d) Energy Consumption

The energy consumption associated with running a blockchain network can be significant, depending on the consensus algorithm used, making it challenging to operate large-scale IoT networks with a significant number of nodes. "Proof of work" consensus algorithms, such as the one used by Bitcoin, consume large amounts of energy because they require significant computational power. Whereas "proof of stake" consensus algorithms, such as the one used by Ethereum, consume relatively less energy, as they do not require intensive computations.

7.4 Adoption of Blockchain Technology in Data science:

Undoubtedly, Data Science is one of the most trending topics in the world today. From businesses to governments, everyone is looking for ways to make better use of data. After all, Data Science can help organizations better understand their customers, optimize their operations, and make better decisions. On the other hand, the popularity of Blockchain technology is on the rise as more and more businesses are beginning to explore its potential uses. Blockchain is a distributed database that allows for secure, transparent, and tamper-proof record-keeping, making Blockchain an ideal technology for a broad range of applications, from financial services to supply chain management. It first gained prominence as the underlying technology behind Bitcoin but has since been adapted for many other use cases.

The combination of Data Science and Blockchain technology is often referred to as "data-driven innovation". This term refers to the use of Data Science techniques to drive the development of new Blockchain-based applications. When these two fields are combined, they can create a "trust-less" system where transactions are verified and recorded without the requirement for a central authority. This combination could have enormous implications for everything from financial sectors to supply chains. By combining Data Science and Blockchain, we can create a more efficient, secure, and transparent world.

7.4.1 Applications of Data Science to Blockchain Technology

There are several potential applications of Data Science to Blockchain technology, and we are just beginning to scratch the surface of what is possible. A few standard applications include:

a)   Facilitates Data Traceability

Blockchain facilitates peer-to-peer collaborations. Any peer can study the entire process and identify how the findings were attained if a published report, for example, fails to explain any approaches sufficiently. Thanks to the ledger's open channels, anyone can understand whether data is accurate, how to keep it, how to update it, where it comes from, and how to use it correctly. Finally, blockchain technology will enable users to trace data from beginning to end.

b)   Ensures High Data Quality and Accuracy

The data in Blockchain's digital ledger is stored in various nodes, together with private and public. The information is cross-checked and analyzed at the entry point before being added to different blocks. This process in and of itself is a means of data verification.

c) Enables Real-Time Data Analysis

Real-time data analysis is highly challenging and being able to watch events in real-time is the most effective method of detecting scammers. On the other hand, real-time data analysis was not possible for a long time. Because of Blockchain's decentralized structure, businesses can immediately notice any abnormalities in the datasets right away.

d) Guarantees Trust

Biases are widespread when there is only one authority. Putting too much trust in one person might be risky. Several firms refuse to provide third parties access to their information due to trust issues. As a result, sharing information becomes practically impossible.

When employing Blockchain technology, the issue of trust is no longer a barrier to information sharing. Businesses can engage more effectively by sharing the knowledge at their disposal.

e) Boosts Data Integrity

Organizations gather data from multiple sources. So, even data acquired from government agencies or developed on the ground can be inaccurate. Furthermore, information from other sources, such as social media may be inaccurate.

Data scientists are now incorporating Blockchain technology to ensure data authenticity and traceability across the chain. One of the reasons for its extensive adoption is its immutable security. Multiple signatures on the Blockchain's decentralized record protect data at every step. For anyone to access the data, valid signatures must be provided. As a result, data breaches and hacking are becoming less common.

Test your Skills

1. Write the advantages for the integration of blockchain technology with cloud computing.

2. Discuss the various characteristics of blockchain technology and cloud computing.

3. How is cloud computing helpful for blockchain applications?

4.   Can we use blockchain technology with artificial intelligence? Justify your answer.

5.   What are the challenges if we integrate blockchain with AI?

6.   Discuss the common Use cases of blockchain and AI

7.   Discuss the potential applications of data science with blockchain technology.

8.   Describe the adoption of blockchain technology in data science.

9.   Write about the promise of blockchain technology in IoT applications.

10.   Can we integrate blockchain technology into IoT applications?

11.   Can we use IoT infrastructure in blockchain applications?

GLOSSARY

Altcoins

Altcoins are Bitcoin alternatives. Altcoins are post-Bitcoin cryptocurrencies. Other cryptocurrencies are called altcoins.

ASIC

An "application-specific integrated circuit" is a silicon chip built for a particular application. ASICs are considered to be much more efficient than conventional hardware (CPUs and GPUs).

Bitcoin

Bitcoin is a cryptocurrency that runs on a (1) global peer to peer network, (2) decentralized (no single entity can control it), (3) open-source (wallet & transaction verification), (4) bypassing middlemen or central authority, with (5) no issuer or acquirer, (6) anyone with a computer or smartphone can use it

Bitcoin ATM

A Bitcoin ATM is an Internet-connected kiosk where clients may buy bitcoin and/or other cryptocurrencies. A cashpoint where people can trade fiat currency and bitcoins

Blockchain

A blockchain is a secured, shared, and distributed ledger that helps the process of recording and tracking assets without the need for a centralized, trusted authority.

Block

A block is a single unit of the blockchain. Its content data is permanently. The consensus mechanism should verify a block before adding it to the blockchain.

Block explorer

A block explorer is a digital tool that enables users to examine information regarding transactions, blocks, addresses, and other activity within a blockchain.

Block reward

The block reward is an incentive offered to miners or validators who successfully add a new block of transactions to the blockchain.

Chain linking

Chain linking in blockchain refers to the process of cryptographically linking each new block to the preceding block, resulting in a continuous, unbreakable sequence or "chain" of blocks. This structure is essential for blockchain's security and immutability.

Client

A client is the software that enables users to interact with the blockchain network. It links to other nodes in the network, allowing users to send transactions, query data, and, in certain cases, mine or validate blocks. Clients are required for accessing and using blockchain networks

Cloud Mining

Cloud mining enables users to mine digital currencies/cryptocurrencies without the need to install, operate, or maintain any mining infrastructure. Users rent computer capacity from a cloud mining operator, who operates massive data centers that are specifically designed for mining, rather than constructing their own mining rigs.

Consensus

Consensus is the mechanism by which a network of nodes agrees on the validity of transactions and the state of the blockchain. This agreement mechanism ensures that all nodes in a decentralized system have the same copy of the ledger and can trust the data without relying on a central authority. Consensus mechanisms are critical for blockchain security because they prevent double-spending and network threats.

Consortium blockchains

A consortium blockchain (also known as a federated blockchain) is a type of private or permissioned blockchain in which multiple organizations or groups govern the network together.

Cryptographic Hash Function

A cryptographic hash function (CHF) is a mathematical function that maps a variable-length data set to a fixed-length bit string, known as a hash value. Modern information security practices use CHFs to secure sensitive data, including passwords.

Crypto jacking

Crypto jacking is a malware that infects a mobile device or computer and then uses techniques to mine cryptocurrency. Malicious crypto mining, also known as crypto jacking, is a threat that infiltrates a computer or mobile device and exploits its resources to crypto mine.

dApp (decentralized application)

Decentralized applications (dApps) are programs that operate on a decentralized network instead of a singular computer or server. Decentralized applications (dApps) function on a blockchain or decentralized network.

DAOs (Decentralized Autonomous Organization)

A blockchain governance system known as a decentralized autonomous organization (DAO) distributes decision-making, management, and entity ownership. DAO is an organization that operates on blockchain technology, guided by code, smart contracts, and consensus rather than a central authority. Participants in a DAO share governance, collectively making decisions on key operations, development, and Treasury management. DAOs aim to enable transparent, trustless, and community-driven decision-making without centralized leadership.

Digital Signature

Digital signatures are used in cryptography to verify the validity and authenticity of digital documents, messages, or transactions. Digitally, it serves the same purpose as a stamped seal or handwritten signature: to verify the authenticity and authenticity of a communication or document.

Double Spending

Double-spending is spending the same cryptocurrency or blockchain token more than once. A potential flaw in digital currency systems is that they allow the spending of a single digital token or cryptocurrency more than once.

Ethereum

Ethereum is a platform for developing and deploying decentralized apps (dApps) and smart contracts. It is open-source.

Ethereum Virtual Machine (EVM)

The *Ethereum Virtual Machine (EVM)* is *a decentralized computing environment that executes smart contracts on the Ethereum Work.* Designed to provide a consistent, reliable, and secure platform for code execution, it is a key component of the Ethereum blockchain, enabling developers to run decentralized applications (dApps) on the Ethereum network.

Fiat currency

Any money declared by a government to be to be valid for meeting a financial obligation, like Rupee, USD. and EUR etc.

Fork

Different parts of the network simultaneously create two blocks, resulting in an ongoing alternative version of the blockchain. This process generates two parallel blockchains, with one of them emerging as the winner.

Genesis block

A blockchain adds additional blocks to the Genesis Block, also known as Block 0. The previous block hash value is denoted 000000#.

Hashcash

Hashcash is a proof-of-work algorithm that has been used as a denial-of-service countermeasure technique in a number of systems.

Halving

In blockchain, the term "halving" refers to a situation when miners' incentive for validating transactions is cut in half, especially when discussing cryptocurrencies like Bitcoin.

Light Node

On a blockchain network, a computer employs the simplified payment verification (SPV) mode to verify only a restricted number of transactions pertinent to its operations.

Lightning Network

Lightning is a decentralized network using smart contract functionality in the blockchain to enable instant payments across a network of participants.

Merkle Tree

A Merkle tree, commonly referred to as a hash tree, serves as a data structure for data verification and synchronization. This data structure serves as a generalization of the hash list. It is a tree structure in which each leaf node is a hash of a block of data, and each non-leaf node is a hash of its children.

Mining

The process of verifying and appending new transactions to a blockchain ledger is known as mining. Proof-of-work (PoW) cryptocurrencies primarily use this fundamental mechanism.

Mining Difficulty

Mining difficulty measures how challenging it would be to find the next Bitcoin block. Every proof-of-work consensus algorithm has a mining difficulty that is also adjustable. Depending on how many miners join the network, the difficulty might rise or fall.

Node (Full Node)

Any operational electronic device that keeps a copy of the blockchain and, frequently, helps with transaction processing is referred to as a node in a blockchain network. A node that downloads and validates the complete blockchain ledger, from the genesis block (the first block) to the most recent block, is known as a full node.

Private Blockchains

On a private blockchain, one organization controls write permissions. Read permissions might be limited or public.

Private key

A private key, also referred to as a confidential key, is a variable that can be used to encrypt and decrypt data. It is confidential and should only be disclosed to the key's generator or parties that are authorized to decrypt the data.

Proof of Authority (PoA)

A proof of authority is a consensus mechanism in a private blockchain that essentially gives one client (or a specific number of clients) with one particular private key the right to make all of the blocks in the blockchain.

Proof of Stake

Proof of Stake (PoS) is a type of algorithm that aims to achieve distributed consensus in a blockchain. A blockchain protocol provides traders with incentives to validate transactions by rewarding them with cryptocurrency for every correct validation. Proof-of-stake protocols safeguard against fraud by requiring traders to "stake" some of their cryptocurrency as collateral, which they then lock up in a deposit. If a trader adds a transaction to the blockchain that other validators deem to be invalid, they can lose a portion of what they staked.

Proof of Work

The Proof of Work (PoW) consensus algorithm involves solving a computationally challenging puzzle in order to create new blockchain blocks. A blockchain network first applies the Proof of Work (PoW) approach to achieve consensus.

Public Blockchains

A public blockchain is one that is open to everyone, allowing individuals to read, send, and anticipate the inclusion of their valid transactions. Furthermore, the consensus process that decides which blocks are incorporated into the chain and the current state is accessible to everyone.

SHA (Secure Hash Algorithm)

Secure Hash Algorithms, also known as SHA, are a family of cryptographic functions designed to keep data secured. It works by transforming the data using a hash function, an algorithm that consists of bitwise operations, modular additions, and compression functions. The hash function then produces a fixed-size string that looks nothing like the original. Once these algorithms transform into their respective hash values, reverting back to the original data becomes nearly impossible. SHA-1, SHA-2, and SHA-3 are a few algorithms of interest, each designed with increasingly stronger encryption in response to hacker attacks.

Smart contracts

Smart contracts are computer protocols that facilitate, verify, or enforce the negotiation or performance of a contract or obviate the need for a contractual clause. Smart contracts typically feature a user interface and frequently mimic the logic of contractual clauses. Thus, proponents of smart contracts assert that they can make many types of contractual clauses partially or fully self-executing, self-enforcing, or both. Smart contracts aim to provide security superior to traditional contract law and to reduce other transaction costs associated with contracting.

Solidity

Solidity is a programming language designed for developing smart contracts. Its syntax is similar to that of JavaScript, and it is intended to compile into bytecode for the Ethereum Virtual Machine (EVM)

SPV (Simplified Payment Verification) client

SPV clients are Bitcoin lightweight clients which do not download and store the whole blockchain locally. These wallets provide a way to verify payments without having to download the complete blockchain. An SPV client only downloads the block headers by connecting to a full node

State Channel

State channels are interactions which get conducted off the blockchain without significantly increasing the risk of any participant. Moving these interactions off of the chain without requiring any additional trust can significantly improve cost and speed. State channels work by locking part of the blockchain state so that a specific set of participants must completely agree with each other to update it

Token

Tokens are assets in the blockchain ecosystem that facilitate the efficient and secure transfer, storage, and verification of information and value.

Tokenization

Tokenization is the process of creating a digital representation of a real thing. Tokenization can also be used to protect sensitive data.

Transaction Fees

Transaction fees serve two essential purposes when it comes to blockchain networks. They reward miners or validators who help confirm transactions.

Turing completeness

A machine is Turing complete if it can perform any calculation that any other programmable computer is capable of. All modern computers are Turing-complete in this sense. The Ethereum Virtual Machine (EVM), which runs on the Ethereum blockchain is Turing complete. Thus it can process any "computable function". It is, in short, able to do what you could do with any conventional computer and programming language

Wallet

Wallets are just like your account number, but the difference is that they let you store the cryptocurrency. It can support single or multiple cryptocurrencies. Wallet can Hot wallet, soft wallet, cold wallet, and Hardware wallet.

51% attack

A 51% attack is an attack on a blockchain network where a single entity gains control of more than half (51%) of its staking or computational power.

MODEL QUESTIONS

1. Discuss the history and evolution of blockchain technology, from its early years to its current state.

2. Define blockchain technology and explain how it differs from traditional databases.

3. Compare and contrast smart contracts with traditional paper-based contracts.

4. What are the key characteristics of blockchain technology?

5. Explain the concept of decentralization in blockchain and its advantages.

6. Why is Byzantine Fault Tolerance important in distributed systems?

7. How does the Byzantine Generals' Problem relate to blockchain technology?

8. What is a smart contract, and how does it work?

9. How does automation in smart contracts reduce the need for intermediaries?

10. Explain the differences between structured and unstructured overlay networks in blockchain.

11. What is the role of cryptographic hash functions in blockchain security?

12. What is the difference between Bitcoin and blockchain?

13. Explain the structure of a blockchain and how blocks are linked.

14. What is a genesis block in a blockchain, and why is it important?

15. Describe the role of consensus mechanisms in blockchain.

16. Describe the process of blockchain mining and the different types of mining.

17. What is a smart contract, and how does it enhance blockchain applications?

18. Differentiate between public and private blockchains with examples.

19. What is a permissioned blockchain, and how does it differ from a permissionless blockchain?

20. Explain the workflow of a smart contract with an example.

21. How does the integration of blockchain and cloud computing improve security and transparency?

22. Explain the major differences between blockchain and cloud computing in terms of data storage and security.

23. What are the advantages of using blockchain for decentralized cloud storage?

24. What is a 51% attack, and how does it threaten blockchain security?

25. How can blockchain enhance the security of Artificial Intelligence (AI) applications?

26. Describe the role of AI in improving blockchain efficiency and automation.

27. What are some key challenges faced when integrating AI with blockchain?

28. How does blockchain improve data privacy and security in AI applications?

29. Explain the role of cryptography in securing blockchain transactions.

30. What are some real-world applications of blockchain in the Internet of Things (IoT)?

31. Explain how blockchain can help address security concerns in IoT networks.

32. What is Sybil Attack in blockchain, and how can it be prevented?

33. What challenges exist when integrating blockchain with IoT in terms of scalability and interoperability?

34. How do consensus mechanisms impact the scalability and efficiency of blockchain networks?

35. How does Byzantine Fault Tolerance improve blockchain scalability?

36. Compare and contrast Proof of Work (PoW) and Proof of Stake (PoS) in terms of energy consumption and scalability in IoT applications.

37. Explain how blockchain enhances transparency and accountability in different industries.

38. How can businesses use smart contracts to reduce operational costs?

39. Discuss the advantages and challenges of implementing blockchain in financial transactions.

40. What are the real-world applications of Byzantine Fault Tolerance beyond blockchain?

41. How can Byzantine Fault Tolerance be improved for future blockchain networks?

42. How can blockchain applications be secured against malware and hacking threats?

43. Discuss the measures that can be taken to improve the security of blockchain applications in financial transactions.